PLANNING CLOUD-BASED DISASTER RECOVERY FOR DIGITAL ASSETS

**Recent Titles in Libraries Unlimited's
Innovative Librarian's Guide Series**

PLANNING CLOUD-BASED DISASTER RECOVERY FOR DIGITAL ASSETS

The Innovative Librarian's Guide

Robin M. Hastings

INNOVATIVE LIBRARIAN'S GUIDE

LIBRARIES UNLIMITED™

An Imprint of ABC-CLIO, LLC

Santa Barbara, California • Denver, Colorado

Library of Congress Cataloging in Publication Control Number: 2017041185

ISBN: 978-1-4408-4238-2 (paperback)
        978-1-4408-4239-9 (ebook)

22   21   20   19   18   1   2   3   4   5

This book is also available as an eBook.

Libraries Unlimited
An Imprint of ABC-CLIO, LLC

ABC-CLIO, LLC
130 Cremona Drive, P.O. Box 1911
Santa Barbara, California 93116-1911
www.abc-clio.com

This book is printed on acid-free paper ∞

Manufactured in the United States of America

Contents

Acknowledgments

As always, any book is a work of a bunch of different people making my work possible. Thanks to the Northeast Kansas Library System (NEKLS) staff for their patience as I took random days off to work on this stuff and for being sounding boards when necessary! Thanks also to my family, including my new husband who got to deal with the crazy of wedding planning while writing a book—thanks for your patience, Mike!

Introduction

Disaster planning has been necessary for as long as there have been disasters. The amount of information about how to plan, what to plan for, and what to do with the plan once a disaster happens is plentiful—almost too plentiful. What this book will do is to take those long-tested best practices for disaster planning, ones that have been refined by time, and put them in a modern, cloud-based context.

Most disaster plans you find on the Internet today assume that you have all your important documents on paper, so copying and storing multiple copies of your insurance policies and personnel records and financial records is a major step in most disaster planning guides. This is changing, though, and many of us now have our documents stored on file servers or individual computers in our organizations. This makes copying and protecting easier—but only if we do it in a systematic and organized way.

For the purposes of this book, cloud-based technology will be loosely defined as "server space or application services that are not based in your organization." The essence of the cloud is that no one should care much about where the information and applications used actually live. It's just "out there" somewhere. Of course, for truly comprehensive disaster planning, you do want to know where your data and applications are being stored so that you can choose multiple locations across the country for their storage. If a hurricane hits Florida and all your data were in a server farm in Miami, you might have a problem. Multiple data farms in use in multiple areas of the country keep your data safe—sort of a large-scale LOCKSS (Lots of Copies Keep Stuff Safe) solution. For the most part, though, and for the purposes of this book unless indicated otherwise, "cloud-based" means not in your building or office space.

Also for the purposes of this book, the definition of "digital assets" will be pretty much anything that isn't on paper. This can be documents, databases, and applications—along with anything else that requires a computer to access or use it. A library's digital assets can include both administrative assets—financial data, insurance papers, documents of any kind, really—and materials. Saving physical assets (such as the books owned by the library or the actual computers used to access and use the library's digital assets) is beyond the scope of this book. There are a number of resources for physical preservation of library spaces and assets—in this book, the focus will be on the preservation of the library's computer and network-based "stuff."

ORGANIZATION OF THE BOOK

This book is organized in a linear fashion: after the introductory material in Chapters 1 and 2, the rest of the book proceeds along the path of creating, testing, and using a disaster plan. Chapters 3 through 5 hold the meat of the book. In Chapter 3, the process of planning, how to put together a team to help plan, and what to consider when starting the plan are all covered. Chapter 4 deals with the tools you will use as part of your plan—the cloud-based services that will help protect your digital assets in each step of the way. From preventing a disaster (as much as we humans can) to detecting that a disaster has happened (surprisingly hard for technology-based disasters, sometimes) to recovering from the disaster, the tools you need to make your plan work will be laid out with suggestions for how to use them well. Chapter 5 then goes into the details of creating the physical plan, now that you have done the thinking work and the evaluation of tools work this chapter helps with the putting together of a set of documents that will help others understand your plan and how to use it. Templates and general forms for your disaster plan are included in this section of the book. Chapters 6 and 7 will help you evaluate your disaster plan by laying out what makes for a good plan and how to test yours to make sure it fits those criteria. Chapter 8 wraps up the information in the previous chapters into a summary of how to deal with the plan after you have created it. Finally, there are appendixes in the back with checklists to use during the planning stages as well as during the evaluating cloud services stages. Those will be available on the web for you to print and make use of as well.

HOW TO USE THE BOOK

You can dip into and out of the book as needed, certainly. If you have a decent plan in place and just want to be sure that you are protecting your digital assets properly, Chapters 4 and 6 might be just what you need. If your organization has no real plan in place, however, reading through the book in order will give you a strong grounding for planning, creating, testing, and making your disaster plan useful for when the worst happens.

No matter where you are in the process of planning for disaster at your library, this book will give you concrete guidance for the process itself as well as ideas for how to manage both the process of planning and maintaining that plan using convenient and relatively inexpensive cloud technologies. As the use of the cloud grows in libraries, you will undoubtedly find new uses and features of cloud computing that will assist you in your planning and carrying out of those plans during a disaster. Disaster planning is becoming more and more necessary as the world changes, and having a good, solid, usable plan in place is becoming more of a requirement for every library. Let this book help you protect your materials, facilities, and, most importantly, staff in the event that the worst should happen!

Chapter 1

What Is a Disaster?

Generally, disasters seem to be pretty noticeable. Natural disasters such as tornadoes, hurricanes, earthquakes, and floods are hard to miss. There are other kinds of disasters, though, that those of us in libraries need to consider when putting together a complete disaster plan. For a small library, a hard drive crash or an accidental leaking of patron data can be a pretty big disaster. To properly plan for and manage disasters, we need to consider what constitutes a disaster.

Many disasters are actually pretty small and easy to miss. Someone hacking into your server to use it as a way to serve illegal files (pirated movies, software, etc.) can go unnoticed until the government notices and comes in to take your server—as well as all the data, software, and everything else stored on that machine—as evidence in a crime. If you don't have a plan to deal with the loss of that server—for whatever reason—you have a disaster on your hands from which you might find it hard to recover.

The scenario above has actually happened and if the library in question hadn't had good backups, a spare server sitting around that could be pressed into service and a staff who could recreate the server and get it back into action quickly, the situation could have been, well, disastrous. Of course, if the library had been practicing good detection such as server monitoring, it might not have happened at all. A big part of disaster planning is figuring out what disasters might happen in your library and how to avoid them. The disaster that doesn't happen doesn't have to be dealt with, after all.

Many disasters, however, cannot be avoided. That tornado bearing down on your building can't be persuaded to change its course, no matter how much planning and detecting of risks you do. Non-natural disasters, though, could be stopped in their tracks by the application of a good disaster recovery plan. Even if the disaster can't be stopped completely, the risks the disaster can pose can be sharply mitigated with some forethought and some planning. This is the intention behind the project management concept of Risk Mitigation—risks that are thought of and planned for will have considerably fewer consequences, or at least less severe consequences, than risks that no one thought of and no one took any steps to mitigate.

In general, a disaster is anything that interrupts the normal flow of your business or organization. For libraries, that is anything from providing materials for patrons to providing information via telephone, Internet, and in person. If you can't perform your mission-critical processes, you have a disaster on your hands. A disaster does not have to be the complete destruction of your facility—it can just be an event or incident that makes provision of service impossible.

In this section, we will consider what makes a disaster and how a library can tell if a disaster of that sort is happening.

TECHNOLOGICAL DISASTERS

Some tech disasters that have happened in libraries I have worked in over the years include:

- Power outages
- Hacking
- Virus outbreak
- Hard drive crash
- Database corruption
- Network failure
- Building (and wiring) damaged by a car hitting the library (surprisingly common, actually)
- Privacy breach/information leak
- Public relations (PR) issues with filtering
- PR issues with ill-advised social media posting
- Abrupt loss of IT staff

Your library does not have to be destroyed for a disaster to have happened. Technological disasters can be much more subtle and even harder to recover from than a big, obvious disaster. If your systems get hacked and nobody notices for a month or two, backups and other risk mitigation strategies that are in place may be useless. If all the data is already corrupted, it can't be just put back into place once the hacked machine or machines are replaced. Other kinds of technological disasters, from a necessary service going offline, an upstream Internet Service Provider's (ISP's) cable being cut, or power outages, are even more frustrating to deal with because you have no control over if and when that service will be restored. Considering how to deal with technologically based services going away—everything from online databases to the library's Internet service to e-mail—even temporarily, should be part of the thinking involved in creating a disaster plan.

A less obvious tech disaster can be the loss of your IT staff. Whether the IT staff leaves under good conditions or not, your library will have to deal with changing passwords and remote access and keeping things going with less staff than you had before. If the IT person leaves under bad circumstances, the issues can be even more serious—you have to worry about sabotage and deliberate damage done to your systems before this person left. Even if the circumstances of an IT person leaving are ideal, the results can be as damaging as a virus in your organization. Your disaster recovery plan should also take into account the various parts of the network and technological environment that your IT staff cover and have some kind of contingency plan for when one of them leaves.

CASE STUDY: SONY SERVERS HACKED

One technology disaster that made worldwide headlines was the Sony e-mail hacking incident. Sony's servers were hacked and private, sometimes sensitive, e-mails were leaked to news agencies around the world. This sort of thing constitutes a couple of different kinds of disasters. First, you have the data breach of the original attack to contend with; then it is followed up by a PR disaster that results from e-mails that people thought were private made public. As a side note, you should never assume your e-mails are private for this reason, among several others.

While this was a big breach and made big headlines, the fact is that only 25 percent of data breaches come from external threats, as the one in the Sony case did. Thirty-one percent of breaches are caused by the loss of a device or laptop that is then exploited for data, with another 27 percent coming from unintentional misuse of data by employees. Only 12 percent came from intentional and malicious misuse of data from insiders, but that happens as well. Beyond securing your data from the outside world, your library should also take steps to make sure your data is protected when on laptops and devices and that your staff are educated on how to handle sensitive financial or patron data as they work. Those two steps alone can alleviate 58 percent of the data breaches that might cause a disaster in your library. The other 25 percent of breaches that come from outside also need to be considered, but good security practices by your staff will help keep the bad guys out too (Prince, 2012).

PERSONNEL DISASTERS

Personnel disasters can be equally hard to deal with, such as:

- Staff having an extended illness
- Staff unexpectedly leaving the library altogether
- Disgruntled staffers with access to technology

Considering what the consequences are for each of these disaster scenarios will help keep your library from suffering some of the worst effects of these disasters.

For disasters that involve key staff being gone for an unexpected, extended period of time, or in the worst-case scenario, not coming back at all, documentation is key. Passwords, service logins, and other information about work being done should be stored in a place that everyone can access and information about work-in-progress projects should be easily accessible for the staff who are picking up the slack. This is where the cloud services that exist to allow people to save—and share—this kind of information are particularly useful. Something like the popular password protection service LastPass (www.lastpass.com) allows staff to save passwords in a shared environment that gives granular control to who has access to what password/login information. If your staff already do much of their work in something like Google Docs or Microsoft's OneDrive, you already have the information about works in progress shared among staff and don't have to worry so much about who has what version of important documents.

Personnel information is a particular issue with disaster recovery planning because the information contained in people's work records is particularly sensitive. Bits of information like social security numbers and other identity information have to be both protected from misuse and loss—and those priorities are often competing. With the concept of making many copies of data to keep it safe, you run the risk of one of those copies getting released out into the world and endangering the identities of your staff. Chapter 2 will have further information on the concept of LOCKSS—Lots of Copies Keep Stuff Safe. Keep all that information in file cabinets in an office in your building, however, and you run the risk of losing it all in a fire or tornado. Risk assessment and management are big keys in managing personnel data and protecting it in the case of either natural or technological disaster. For more on risk management, see the section on "Risk Assessment and Management" in Chapter 4 of this book.

TRADITIONAL DISASTERS

What most people traditionally think of when they think of disasters are:

- Natural disasters such as tornadoes, earthquakes
- Fire
- Floods

These can wipe out both the physical facilities and technology resources of a library. This is where having a plan for more than just the recovery of the library's technology is important. Your disaster plan should just be a part of what you put together to deal with disasters and other events that disrupt the library. You also need to worry about how you will continue doing business, as a library, after a disaster—this means knowing where and how important documents (insurance, financial records, personnel records, just to name a few) are stored as well as plans for what to do with the business side of the library in the case of a disaster. See the section on "Business Continuity Plan" for more information.

Planning for technology in the face of a natural disaster is necessary, though. Things like fire alarms and other warning systems can help reduce the amount of damage done by a fire by catching it quickly. Other things, like building wide sprinkler systems that automatically come on when they detect smoke, can prove to be as harmful (if not more) than the fire itself because neither servers nor books do well when doused with lots of water. While fires can happen anywhere at any time, other natural disasters may be more or less likely to happen in your library's geographical area. If you are in the Midwest of the United States, you might get a big band of rain as a result of a hurricane hitting elsewhere in the country, but are unlikely to have the full effects of a hurricane like you might if your library was located in Florida or on the Gulf Coast. Conversely, those libraries located in the desert Southwest are unlikely to need to have a plan in place for a tornado, but might want to consider what to do if an earthquake should hit. A disaster that is a bit less traditional in the Midwest, but something the west coast might need to consider would be a tsunami. Libraries in Hawaii should definitely have this on their minds as they consider their disaster plans! Related to that would be flooding and blizzard conditions that could cause damage to the library in many different ways.

There are many different kinds of natural disasters—from comet strikes to trees falling on the building or the wires connecting the building with power and Internet access—but each of them has the potential to take out the library's technology in many different ways.

OTHER DISASTERS

Public Relations

There are a number of other things that can happen in a library that could fall under the "disaster" label. One of those things is a disaster of public relations—having something happen at the library that casts a bad light on the organization and/or staff. While this kind of disaster may not be the first that comes to mind when thinking of disaster recovery and cloud-based tools, there are ways to help mitigate even PR disasters using the cloud. With this kind of disaster, the inability for the organization to be able to provide service—phone lines are tied up, staff are unable to perform their duties, or the PR disaster is so bad that the organization no longer has the trust of the community—is not of the traditional "things are broken or inaccessible" type, but a more subtle kind of inability to do the job of the library.

Social Media

Social media can be both the cause of and remedy for a library disaster. A rogue employee firing off an ill-considered tweet or Facebook post can cause huge rifts between the community and the library. Training and well-considered policies can head some of those disasters off before they affect your library. Having good limits on who is able to post to each social media account the library runs is helpful, too. Mostly, having a plan to react properly and respond intelligently to a social media/PR disaster is the way to help mitigate that risk.

The ease of spreading news via social media can be another way a library could find itself facing a disaster. It seems like at least once a month, another news story about "weeding gone wild" ends up in the news. Because snapping a picture and posting it to social media is easy, people can spread the word that a local library is getting rid of books at the speed of light, it seems. Once a story like that is out and the local (taxpaying) populace is aroused, the library will find itself facing a PR disaster that it will have to confront, counter, and quell.

Funding

Another type of disaster that could hit a library is a funding crunch. Many libraries had their budgets slammed during the most recent recession and some have not yet recovered. This necessitates thinking about paying for required services and materials (including technology equipment) in a way that is very much like figuring out how to recover from any other kind of disaster. Sometimes the disastrous funding situation is slow enough to emerge that the library can plan ahead enough to mitigate the damages, sometimes it is not. For those times when the funding issues are sudden and severe, disaster recovery plans could provide some guidance on the most mission-critical technology that the library must keep running and the not-so-critical technology that the library could let slide until the funding situation improves.

Humans

Finally, there are all the various "human-caused" disasters that can happen—simple errors that take down a server, burglary and embezzlement, vandalism, and various kinds of computer crimes. These disasters can cause other kinds of disasters to happen—a public charge of embezzlement can lead to a PR issue if the community doesn't believe the library is a good steward of their tax dollars. While other kinds of human disasters—active shooters, bomb threats, and the like—may not directly affect technology (unless that bomb goes off, of course), these kinds of things are still important to consider in the larger business continuity plan (BCP), if not the disaster plan itself.

HOW TO PLAN FOR THE UNKNOWN

Planning for something that you don't know will happen can be tricky. First you have to figure out what might happen—all the things that might happen—then rate them by likelihood. As mentioned above, you might consider that a tornado might take out your library building, but if you are in the northern Midwest where blizzards are much more likely, you need not spend a lot of time planning for a tornado-based disaster and rather spend your time considering what to do if a blizzard takes out the power system, the roof, or the roads leading to your library.

Planning for the unknown requires a few steps and some imagination. For natural disasters, you can use the historical record of your area to determine what might be most likely to affect your library. For other kinds of disasters, you may need to do some creative brainstorming, since disasters like a PR mess up or a hard drive crash may have never happened at your organization, but could happen in the future. For disasters relating to people—personnel disasters or a PR flub—you can learn from others who have gone through a similar incident to help guide your list of possible disasters and the steps needed to take care of them.

A brainstorming session with lots of brains involved to come up with ideas is a great way to come up with a list of disasters that might happen. As those ideas start flowing, more will be triggered and, with enough time and creativity, you will find a pretty decent list of possible disasters you might encounter. Research also helps with this step, as there may be information in magazines and trade journals detailing disasters that other libraries have faced and overcome. Doing some basic research on disasters in libraries before the brainstorming session might help participants get started on the idea generation part of the session more quickly.

To brainstorm effectively, there are some general guidelines that are considered best practices you can follow.

- First is to prepare the group for the session. Make sure they know what the topic is (i.e., possible disasters to hit the library) and what the expectations for the outcome will be.
- Choose a single person to record all the ideas from the session in a place where everyone can see him or her (this makes it easy for participants to see an idea and riff off of it) and make sure the rules for the session are in place before beginning.
- The most common rule for a good brainstorming session is no judgment—allow everyone to express their ideas without anyone making comments, positive or negative.
- Give participants a few moments at the beginning of the session, after the problem and the expectations are laid out, to brainstorm ideas for possible disasters individually. Once that is done, encourage people to give a few of their ideas until the group is spontaneously providing disaster scenarios without prompting.
- Once the session is done, make sure everyone gets a copy of the results and encourage further suggestions for a period of time after they go back to their work.

When you have a number of possible disasters to consider, the next step in the process is ranking them by likelihood. Which are more likely to happen at

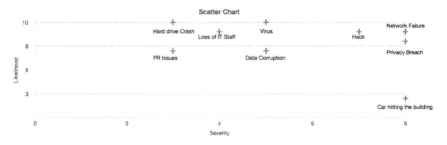

Figure 1.1 Likelihood vs. Severity Chart

your organization and why? One person may suggest a possible disaster, such as a filter failure that causes a PR disaster that is unlikely to happen in your library because you don't use filters. Other disasters (and to be frank—this will be most of them) will be possible, but range on a scale from "will definitely happen at some point" (such as getting a virus in the network) to "possible, but not terribly likely" (such as dealing with the aftermath of a comet strike). One other criterion to consider in this ranking step is the severity of the disaster. If a virus is very likely to happen, but is also very easy to manage, it would have a high likelihood, but a low severity ranking. When you are done, you should have a rough idea of what kind of disasters you should focus on. In the chart shown in Figure 1.1, those would be the ones right at the top, with high likelihood and high severity.

Finally, keeping up with what is going on around you in other libraries—what kinds of disasters they are facing and what they are doing about them is a great way to make sure you are prepared for just about anything. Reading through articles that focus on how libraries came back from a disaster can help you both determine likely disasters and provide some ideas for planning for recovery from them. See the "Resources" section at the back of this book for some articles that have excellent information on how various communities recovered from different kinds of disasters. Knowing your community will help as well. If you are aware of the sentiments of your particular community, you are less likely to end up on the wrong end of a PR disaster than if you don't keep track of the values and mores of your community.

NO PLAN? YOU ARE NOT ALONE

In the Heritage Health Information 2005 report, "A Public Trust At Risk: The Heritage Health Index Report on the State of America's Collections," one of the statistics given for emergency and disaster plans of collecting institutions (museums, libraries, archives) is that only 20 percent have a plan in place and people trained to use it. Note that this report points out that just having a plan isn't enough. Having staff who know what the plan is, where it can be found, and how to make use of it in an emergency is as important as having the plan itself. Planning and forgetting is just as dangerous as not planning at all. The fact that so many of our institutions have no workable plan puts a vast majority of our cultural history—both print and digital—at risk in the event of a disaster. While the planning process is important, this statistic also shows that training for that plan is important as well—the most vital part of any plan is the people who will be implementing it, and if a library's staff aren't familiar with the plan and doesn't know what to do, valuable time (and data) can be lost while the staff try to figure out what they need to do.

BEFORE, DURING, AND AFTER THE DISASTER

Disaster recovery planning is a process. It should, hopefully, start before a disaster occurs and continue to be reviewed and refined until such time a disaster happens—then it should be further refined in light of the issues that come up during the implementation of the plan during the disaster. Disaster planning can be a long process, with lots of moving parts and needing the input of lots of different people, so the best time to start on it is yesterday. Barring that, beginning as soon as possible and then committing to reviewing and testing the plan regularly is your next best bet. The one thing libraries do not want to face is a disaster without a plan in place. That can be costly in terms of both money and time as people scramble to figure out what to do and who should do it.

When beginning the planning process, be sure to look outside your organization as well. Partnerships with police, fire departments, city chambers of commerce, and other related organizations will be helpful. Having best practice guides for your city for police and fire response is useful and those institutions probably have some good advice for you during your planning process. Other organizations that you regularly come into contact with might have some helpful advice or be willing to partner with you when the disaster strikes. Including them in the planning process ensures that you know what community resources you can use when the time comes.

Inside your organization are a number of people who can be useful sources of ideas and information while putting together your plan. Make sure any committee or group that is charged with disaster planning work is as diverse as possible—at least one person from every department or work group should be included to ensure that nothing is missed or forgotten.

One of the things that you can do that can save a lot of money after a disaster is to put together a good list of service providers who are "approved" in advance. After a disaster, scammers and cheats come out of the woodwork and an organization that has no idea what a good data recovery service should cost is at risk of being scammed or cheated by unscrupulous folks willing to take advantage of your immediate need for service. Having a consultant or service in place before an event—one that can be trusted—is an excellent first step to preventing getting robbed after you've just had a disaster!

The plan, just in the process of putting it together, should produce some benefits for your library. First, you can act to prevent some disasters once they've been identified. You can train staff on disaster recovery procedures if you have a working document to train from. You also have the opportunity to get supplies that might be needed to get your technology back up and running—whether that be a generator for emergency power or putting aside an extra server for emergency replacement purposes. You can also take the planning time to assign responsibilities so that everyone knows who needs to do what in the chaotic time after a disaster. Finally you can learn what techniques you need to recover your technology before the disaster happens. The worst time to learn how to do something is in the middle of a stressful time anyway, so making sure that the tools and techniques you need are in place is a huge benefit when the time comes to use them.

After the plan is put together and the committee has produced the final document and distributed it to everyone who needs a copy you can rest—for a short while. The plan should be reviewed and tested regularly and that review and testing process should start within a few months—six at the most—of the end of the document creation process. It should continue, every six months without fail, until a disaster strikes. Every year, at least, a review of the document should be undertaken to ensure that the information is up-to-date. Technology changes fast, and if you can do a review every six months, that would be best, but no more than a year should pass without the document being updated and made current in regards to your technology and human resources.

Considering human resources, do you put in individual names or roles into the plan as you are creating it? That's a decision each library will need to make, but the easiest way to keep a plan up-to-date is to use roles in the body of the plan, but have lists of the people (including outside the library contact information) as the first page or two of the plan itself. It is easier to update a list of people that resides on a sheet of paper you can just update, reprint, and file than to try to find every instance of Barbara's name in the plan and replace it, usually requiring reprinting the whole thing, once Barbara moves on to another position.

Once the disaster is over, and the recovery is starting, there are a few things you should do in order to make sure you recover completely. First thing is to assess the damage—what was damaged and what needs attention first? Can you document the damage (e.g., photos for physical damages to your hardware and equipment, documentation of what was lost for software, and data losses)? Once you know what was damaged, then you can start to work on recovering the most mission-critical systems (the ones that had already been identified by your plan, of course) and start to get back on your feet. During this period, you can decide what equipment can be saved and what needs to be scrapped or replaced.

After a disaster, no matter how small, the group should reconvene to discuss the efficacy of the plan. Some of the questions that are helpful to ask at this point are:

- Did the plan work well?
- Was anything needed that wasn't in the plan?
- Did everyone remember to use the plan?
- How easy was it to access the plan itself and the resources mentioned in the plan?

Whatever might have been missed in the first planning process should be addressed and added to the plan. At this point, you can reset the clock and give yourselves a few months to start the reviewing and testing process again.

BUSINESS CONTINUITY PLAN

Disaster planning and recovery is just part of a larger set of activities that constitute business continuity planning (BCP). Business continuity refers more to retaining or reestablishing business activities (in the case of libraries, checking books in and out, providing services such as reference, etc.) than the more narrowly IT-focused disaster recovery that this book will cover. It encompasses the ability of the organization to continue to deliver services at levels that are defined by the plan itself. Each of the parts of the BCP process is useful for disaster recovery, but most of them are beyond the scope of this book. This introduction to the idea of BCP is included just so readers can get a taste of the full process that disaster recovery fits into. The main concepts of a BCP are:

- Business needs
- Building occupant needs
- Operational needs
- Incident management
- Disaster recovery
- Hot sites and business continuity

While libraries are not businesses, there are enough similarities in libraries to for-profit businesses that considering a full BCP can be advisable for many organizations. While this book will only provide a brief introduction to the concept, there are many resources both in print and on the web that can help guide a library through the planning and creation of a full BCP:

- https://www.ready.gov/business/implementation/continuity
  This is a PDF from the U.S. government that can be used to help your organization plan for successful continuity after a disaster.
- http://www.wikihow.com/Create-a-Business-Continuity-Plan
  This site has 13 steps for creating a successful BCP—many of those steps are

repeated in this book as best practices for the disaster recovery part of the BCP, but they can be expanded to cover more than just the IT portion of disaster recovery.

- http://www.finra.org/industry/small-firm-business-continuity-plan-template
  This is a small-business-oriented template in Word format that can be used to create a BCP for libraries.
- http://en.wikibooks.org/wiki/Business_Continuity_Planning
  Wikibooks has an entry on BCP as an overview.

Business Needs

Business needs encompass everything needed to keep the library running. This can range from satisfying regulatory requirements like document retention to providing phone service so that patrons and customers can contact the library. This also includes the staff of the library—without staff and the ability of staff to get to work and do work while there, the library won't be able to provide service. Consideration of what your human resources will need is a business need as well.

Another set of business needs you should consider are documents needed to get back into business. Financial records and insurance documentation are vital to getting the organization back on its feet, so making sure that the documents you need to get your library back to business are accessible, even if the building is not, is crucial.

To successfully plan to have all business needs met, you need to consider what those needs are for your organization. Brainstorming sessions—as many as needed—would be a good way to make sure all the elements that are necessary are included. Bring in frontline staff as well as administration and write down everything. See the section "How to Plan for the Unknown" above for tips on good brainstorming sessions. It's far better to have to winnow the list down to just pure necessities than to have too few items in the list and miss something critical.

Occupant Needs

Occupant needs are things that your staff and patrons will need before you can be considered recovered. This includes computers on which to work and chairs on which to sit and books for patrons to check out. It also includes basic services like running water, HVAC systems, and a workplace free of mold or other toxic substances. Researching what your local government requires for a safe business place would be a good place to start here—if you can meet those criteria and have the equipment needed for staff to do their work, you can likely be back in business quickly.

There are a couple of issues that need to be considered when thinking of occupant needs. One of those issues is of accessibility. Your secondary site has to be as accessible to the public and your staff as your original site was. Another is the family or contact person for your staff. That information needs to be on hand if something happens and you need to contact someone to inform them of their loved one's condition. Finally, make sure you have plans for every building—evacuation routes, meeting places for after the disaster, and site-specific information for each of your locations.

Operational Needs

Operational needs are those the operations of your business require. This can include items from the business and occupant needs lists given above and much more. One way to determine operational needs before a disaster is to do a working audit. Have staff log what they do (and how they do it—what systems they use on the network, what equipment they use, etc.) for a week or two and use those logs to determine what systems, equipment, and technology is required to keep the library running.

What to consider here is the needs of the organization—what is necessary to the mission and what must be brought back to full operation in order for the library to do its business. One way to do this is to do a business impact analysis (BIA) where you consider, department by department, what the impact of the loss of department functions, applications, and the records kept might be. The Rochester Institute of Technology has a Word document that helps organizations consider those factors in the course of BCP at https://www.rit.edu/fa/buscont/content/operational-recovery.

Incident Management

Incident management refers to the part of the BCP that addresses specifics about how the incident will be handled. This is the part of the plan that includes actions taken—the "who is responsible for what" area. In this section, the plan will break down the likely steps needed to recover the business and assign those actions to particular people or roles in the organization. Some of the actions to be done include communication management, technology management, and document management. For communications, there should be a plan in place to inform staff of what has happened and what they are expected to do (come to work or not, etc.). For technology, each of the IT staff should have specific networks or hardware to check and, if possible, return to service at the end of the disaster. For documents, there should be someone who knows where the important documents are and how they can be accessed in an emergency and, not least, what steps are required to make use of them (in the case of insurance documents, for example, the person responsible will need to contact the agency, provide appropriate documentation, and act as liaison with the agent if necessary).

The hardest part, in some cases, is incident detection. For some incidents, the results are not obvious (see the story of the hacked server in the first section of this chapter) and it can be a while before the incident is noticed if active monitoring isn't going on. Once the incident has been detected, then it must be reported and the procedures to do that are laid out in this section as well.

The bulk of incident management is figuring out the specific steps needed in the immediate aftermath of a disaster incident and clearly writing them down in the documentation. That list is then parceled out to various staff members (or roles, if you have a large turnover and would prefer to say the HR manager does things, as opposed to specifically naming the HR manager in the documentation) so that they have clear and specific directions to follow in the case of an emergency. This information should be clearly communicated and easily accessed by any of the people who need it—one way to make use of the cloud here is to have the document in an off-site storage service (Google Docs, Dropbox, Box.net, etc.) so that any computer or mobile device with Internet access will be able to get to it.

Disaster Recovery

Finally, disaster recovery is the final part of a BCP and specific details on how to plan for disaster recovery will constitute the rest of this book. As a quick overview, however, the disaster recovery part of a plan consists of making sure the organization's technology and technological capabilities are recovered. This includes every part of an organization's tech, from phone and power service, recovering data on individual computers, to making sure the organization's server resources are brought back online. Disaster recovery includes monitoring for disasters, responding to disaster incidents, and recovering the technology affected after a disaster.

HOT SITES AND BUSINESS CONTINUITY

One concept that comes up frequently in business continuity planning is the idea of having a hot site in place—that is a copy of business critical documents, software, and other resources that can be immediately swapped for the resources destroyed or damaged in a disaster. This can be as elaborate as a secondary site with all the technology and resources required to do the work of the organization in place at all times. This can be extraordinarily expensive and isn't something libraries have ever had the resources to consider—in the past. The advent of cloud computing and pay-as-you-go computing resources means that backups can be planned out as "hot sites" themselves, so that in the case of a complete collapse of a library's technology, the backups can be brought online and in use with no more than a 10- or 15-minute window of down time. This changes the concept of backups as passive archives of information to more active repositories of current data that is no more than five minutes out of date in comparison to the currently used technology. With cloud computing, this can be done much more easily and cheaply than ever before.

A more limited version of a hot site is a reserve server or computer that can be hooked up and used to replace a crashed machine in minutes. With the operating system and core software already in place, a reserve machine just needs to have the most recent backup recovered into it to be usefully put into service. The reserve machine doesn't have to be the latest and greatest technology, either it just needs to fill the gap between the current server going offline, for whatever reason, and either that server being recovered and put back into service or a new server being purchased and put into place. It can be an older server that has been retired, but isn't yet completely dead or even a newer computer that is powerful enough to do the job for a while. A traditional hot site, or even a cloud-based hot site, is probably beyond the capabilities and resources of all but the largest libraries, but a reserve machine "hot site" is well within the abilities of even a smallish library.

A DISASTER SUCCESS STORY

Some disasters can be used as an object lesson in what should be done to prepare and to manage during the event. This was the case during a flooding disaster that affected the entire state of Vermont (and beyond, as well, hitting nearly the entire East Coast of the United States) in 2011 during Tropical Storm Irene. All 251 of the state's municipalities were affected by this disaster, with flooding and infrastructure damage common in each one. Wikipedia's entry for the storm (http://en.wikipedia.org/wiki/Hurricane_Irene#Vermont) claims that nearly every river and stream in Vermont flooded and that the cost of damages caused by the storm (in the entire United States, not just Vermont) was the seventh highest in U.S. history. In response to this storm and the damage it caused, the Vermont Council on Rural Development (VCRD), with just 18 months and $1.8M in Federal Disaster Relief Funds, launched the Vermont Digital Economy Project. This project was designed to help communities in Vermont recover their virtual infrastructure from damage done during the storm. The VCRD partnered with a number of community organizations, including libraries, to give out several grants and support many different projects focusing on the state's virtual recovery.

Contained in the final report issued by the project's director, Sharon Combs-Farr, is an interesting nugget for those who are concerned about technological disaster response. She wrote that "the towns with the best virtual infrastructures were both better able to cope with the disaster and also recovered more quickly from it" (VCRD, 2014). That report is available online at http://bit.ly/VDEPreport. While their disaster recovery plans and procedures weren't necessarily focused on cloud-based and virtual disaster planning, such as will be described in this book, they still found a benefit in strong infrastructure and virtual resources while recovering from the storm and the subsequent floods.

While it is sometimes hard to see the good that can be found in a disaster—from the smallest tech glitch to the seventh most expensive disaster in the United States—what this report does in looking back at the disaster and determining the lessons learned in what went wrong and what went right is useful. In the thick of things, it can be hard to figure out just what is working and what isn't. This is why having some kind of "lessons learned" process where the disaster is analyzed and processes and actions are considered is so valuable.

Chapter 2

What Are Cloud-Based Tools?

THE CLOUD

When discussing the use of the cloud with disaster recovery, one of the basic stepping stones is the definition of "the cloud." A cloud is basically any server that isn't in your building. This is a fine and simple definition for most purposes, but since we will be making use of the cloud extensively in later chapters, we should probably expand on that definition now. This can be difficult, because there are several competing definitions. The one that I have used for most nontechnical audiences is that the cloud is any computing resource that you use that is outside of your building or network. That definition is a bit simple, though, because some private clouds (using our second definition, coming up soon) are held entirely within an organization's internal network. For the vast majority of cloud services, however, the definition is apt, if limited.

The second definition involves a bit more technology. The cloud is server resources that are set up to be scalable and moveable without regard to the underlying hardware. This means that whatever software or architecture used to provide the services of the cloud are hardware-agnostic and do not care what server manufacturer or even what collection of parts is used at all. They can move to any other server, with the appropriate operating system, and be immediately in use again as soon as the change is made. This requires some specialized software, often referred to as a stack, that can offer this feature. The other requirement, that it is scalable, means that if necessary, the software can use the resources of several servers at once. For low-volume days, the software may just use a single server, but for high-volume days, multiple servers can be added to handle the load. This involves specialized load balancing software and plenty of planning to make it work, but it is pretty common in many data centers that offer "cloud-based infrastructure" for organizations.

Many private clouds are set up using this kind of technology. Private clouds are servers using cloud software and server architecture that are actually housed in your network. They give some organizations the benefits of the cloud without having to move their data outside their own network and, in the process, giving up some control of both the cloud and the data within it. While most cloud-based hosts and services have clear terms of service that provide protection for internal data, some organizations would prefer not to risk it and keep it all inside, but use those same cloud tools and techniques to get the benefits of scalability and movability in their data centers.

TECH DEFINITION: STACK

From Wikipedia's Solution Stack page (https://en.wikipedia.org/wiki/Solution_stack)—a stack is a set of software components that are used to create a platform that is complete in and of itself. One of the most commonly used software stacks in technology is the LAMP stack—the **L**inux operating system with the **A**pache web server software, the **M**ySQL database software, and the **P**HP web programming software. This stack provides a complete solution to the needs of a standard website developer and is frequently used by web hosts to indicate that all four of those software components are present in their hosting setup. Cloud solutions frequently refer to the stacks that they offer in order to provide a complete infrastructure for their customers.

The third definition of the cloud that we will look at is an official one—from the National Institute of Standards and Technology (NIST). In the NIST Special Publication 800–145 (found at http://csrc.nist.gov/publications/nistpubs/800–145/SP800–145.pdf), the definition of the cloud is:

> Cloud computing is a model for enabling ubiquitous, convenient, on-demand network access to a shared pool of configurable computing resources (e.g., networks, servers, storage, applications, and services) that can be rapidly provisioned and released with minimal management effort or service provider interaction.

That definition also points out that cloud-based services are at least partially automated—end users can add more capabilities to their "clouds" without having to file a ticket and wait for the data center technicians to do the additions. In that same document, NIST identifies five essential characteristics that are required for services to be considered fully cloud-based:

- On-demand self-service (automation)
- Broad network access (accessible through a variety of networked devices)
- Resource pooling (scalability)
- Rapid elasticity (also scalability)
- Measured service (pay by gigabyte (GB) of storage or transfer, rather than flat fees)

To put this all together, we can look at a popular cloud service—Google Docs—to see how it meets those definitions and covers those characteristics.

ON-DEMAND SELF-SERVICE

Anyone can create a Google account and get access to Google Docs through a simple web-based signup form that immediately gives them access to their account with no waiting and no human having to be involved. This requires a way for the technology that Google Docs is based upon to be immediately usable and scalable, since the chances are that many people are adding accounts all the time and running out of server space for a new account would keep the service from being truly cloud-capable, since a human would have to add more server resources. It also requires backend software that allows users on the web to provision space and services for themselves automatically. While the technology for this is beyond the scope of this book, this is a fairly common feature of cloud-based tools and one of the reasons why so many non-IT staff tend to appreciate cloud-based tools like Gmail—it doesn't require prior IT "permission" to use.

BROAD NETWORK ACCESS

As those who have used Google Docs know, one of the major benefits of the service is the fact that you can access it from any computer (or device) with an Internet connection, no matter where you are. The other part of this benefit comes from the ubiquity of Google Docs on devices other than computers. Most of the major phone and tablet operating systems offer a Google Docs app that gives you full read and write access to your Docs from anywhere you happen to be (and with offline access, you don't even need to always have an Internet or data connection, too). Even without a special app, though, the Google Docs service is fully usable with just a browser, so any new devices or mobile systems that come along can still take advantage of Google Docs as long as they include a browser of some sort in their system.

The technology that allows this kind of multi-device use is not really cloud-centric. Any website can be created that works on mobile browsers just by being responsive. Responsive websites not only scale to the size of the screen being used to access them, but they also can reconfigure menus and images so that they work well on both very large and very small screens. This is a web design technique, not a server tool, but it is something that is expected with most cloud-based services, so it merits a mention here.

SCALABILITY

As mentioned in the "On-Demand Self-Service" section, scalability is a requirement for cloud applications. For our purposes, this just means that there are ways to grow the service that don't require a human to add new resources. One other benefit of this is that, in connection with measured service provisions below, cloud services can be very cost-effective in that you pay for what you use and no more. Traditional server-based computing can be wasteful—most of the capabilities of a traditional server go unused most of the time. The capabilities have to be there for the bursts of high traffic during certain parts of the day or during certain events, but the rest of that time, that potential is just sitting there, unused. With a cloud service that is scalable, your organization pays for the server capabilities it uses and no more. When you have low demand (most of the time), the service provided is minimal and cheap. When you have high demand, however, the service is there and it grows as demand does—and then shrinks when the demand is over, making it far more affordable than providing static services that meet high demand, even during low-demand times.

MEASURED SERVICE

As mentioned in the "Scalability" section, measured service means that instead of paying a flat rate for a flat amount of computing power, you are now able to pay for just the power you use and no more. This can mean that your bill fluctuates from month to month, but it generally means that bill is lower than before, when you were paying flat fees each month. Measured service can be measured in a number of ways. The most common are storage, traffic, and computing cycles.

Storage means that you are paying for a particular amount of hard disk space to be made available for you at all times. This is generally part of a measured service plan and usually can be altered "on the fly" (any time you want by just logging into your service dashboard and raising or lowering the amount of storage available to your account). Because the price of hard disk storage is going down precipitously, the cost of storage is usually the smallest part of your costs for cloud services. Gmail still gives away 25 GB of storage for free with every e-mail account—and adding more is pretty inexpensive.

Traffic means that the bandwidth—usually both "up" and "down"—is metered and charged as used. Traffic "up" means traffic from your cloud service to the general web. Every time a web page is requested from a web server, the server sends that page up to the Internet to be delivered. Traffic "down" means traffic from your cloud service from the general web. The request for the page itself is sent down to your server for response. Quite often, traffic up and down will be metered and billed differently, though not always. Sometimes the bill will just be for bandwidth—traffic in both directions—and it won't be separated out. Either way, knowing what kind of traffic you expect will help you choose the right bandwidth package for your needs.

Computing cycles is a charge for actual processor use. Every time a processor is put into service to compute a request or respond to that request, cycles are measured and charged to your account. This kind of measured service is less common in consumer-level cloud services, but more common for developers or enterprise-level cloud services. Again, this is just another way to pay for what you are using, as opposed to paying for a high-priced, high-capacity processor that is very rarely fully used.

WHY IS THE CLOUD NEEDED FOR DR NOW?

When considering why you and your organization might need to use the cloud for disaster recovery now, think about how much of your essential data and services are dependent on technology and a connection to the Internet. Before the computing era, disaster recovery focused on repairing moldy and waterlogged books, keeping collections safe and dry and under a working roof, and recovering paper-based materials after a big natural disaster. As mentioned in the first chapter, with the advent of our dependence on technology, the nature of disasters has changed to include much more than just a natural disaster that occurs every few years, at the most. Now we have so much data, material, and so many services that are technologically based that disaster recovery has come to mean recovering technology in general.

Even in the early days of technology, though, there weren't as many ways to keep data safe and recover vital data as there are now, with the advent of cloud computing in our libraries. We can now store data anywhere in the world and access it in milliseconds—and this has implications for disaster recovery in that there is no need to have our most important documents and collections and services dependent on a single location's ability to be up and accessed. Since we can now spread out our data and make it less vulnerable just by the fact that it's no longer tied to a single location, the cloud can be a real benefit to disaster recovery planners. Many cloud providers advertise that one of their benefits is that their data are mirrored across several different locations, causing that spreading out of data that can keep it safe from natural disasters. Mirroring means that the data on the servers in one place are immediately copied, as soon as they are added or changed, to servers in another place. With cloud services, this place is often geographically distant, giving us some protection from Mother Nature.

LOCKSS AND HOW THE CLOUD CAN HELP

One of the major benefits of a cloud service is that it can allow even the smallest organization to take advantage of the idea of LOCKSS (Lots of Copies Keep Stuff Safe). This concept is one that has been true for many years before the advent of computers and technology. From monasteries that put monks to work copying the classics to the printing press and carbon copies to the modern copier, the idea of making copies to ensure that documents can be accessed, even if the originals are lost, is an old one. For most of history, copying documents was a labor-intensive process, so only the most important were copied. Today, with many of our documents being "born digital," it's as easy as pressing the "Save As" button on your document creation software to create a perfect copy. Even paper documents that have no digital representation can be copied at the press of a button on a copier or scanner.

The cloud service Dropbox (or Box.net—they are very similar) is a perfect example of the LOCKSS principle in action. To use Dropbox, you first sign up for an account. It's free for a 2-GB account, but still pretty cheap for larger storage needs. Once you have an account, you can download the software to your computer (as with many cloud services, this software works with Windows, Mac, and Linux-based operating systems) and install it. Once installed, it can either create a special folder called "Dropbox" or you can point it to an existing folder such as your My Documents folder on a Windows machine. That folder will be the "home" folder for your account. Any item put into that folder will be immediately copied to your cloud-based Dropbox account as long as your Internet connection is on; if not, it will be queued up to be sent (also known as "syncing") as soon as the Internet is available. To create a secondary storage area, such as your home computer, if you are doing this at work, you can download the software to your computer, install it, and create your Dropbox folder on that machine. Within a few minutes—depending on your Internet speed—every document that you have on your home folder on your account will be copied into this secondary computer. This process creates copies—as many as you want depending on the number of computers you attach to your Dropbox account—and makes your digital stuff safe in the process. Even if there is a huge natural disaster that takes out both the library and your home computers, the documents are still safely stored on your Dropbox account server to be instantly downloaded when needed (or accessed from the Dropbox website). If the Dropbox service is the one to encounter a disaster, your documents are still safe on your local computers. This is the essence of LOCKSS.

This principle applies to nondigital items as well. Many public and university libraries have photos and historical documents from their communities for which they act as the repository. If those documents are damaged in a flood, fire, or other disasters, they are often irreplaceable. There are no other copies of those documents floating around to allow the library to reassemble its collection. Digitizing documents, however, can provide some of the benefits of LOCKSS as well as making those items more accessible to the general public. While the items might still be stored in the basement of your building, available to those who are physically close enough to come see them, once digitized, they are not only made safe from natural disasters but are also made available to those who can't come to see them in person. While a digital representation may not be quite as good as seeing the real thing in person, for some items, for others it may satisfy a number of needs for patrons of which you may not even be fully aware.

One such project, Recollections: Kansas (http://www.recollectionsks.org), is an access-level project that helps libraries and communities put their historical images and documents online for the world to see. The Kansas Humanities Council has an excellent program that helps Kansas memory institutions (libraries, museums, archives, etc.) preserve their collections, but the goal of Recollections: Kansas is not necessarily to preserve, but to provide access. Of course, in the process of scanning and digitizing these items for access, some preservation activities are going on as well. Both kinds of digitizing will be covered in the next section.

SCANNING AND DIGITIZING DOCUMENTS NOT "BORN DIGITAL"

Before beginning a scanning project, in order to get your paper documents into a format that can be stored in the cloud, some basic decisions need to be made. For organizational documents (historical records, paper copies of business records, etc.) one of the first things that should be decided is how the documents will be scanned. Format is the first part of that decision. Digital decay occurs when a document is no longer readable or accessible by current software. Many people who have documents in WordPerfect format find that accessing them in the current Microsoft Word environment is difficult—few organizations have the proper software to open and manipulate them. The current standard for cross-compatible document storage is the Adobe PDF format. This is not an open format, but it is a de facto standard and the software to read and write to it is widely available. The Open Document Format (.odf) is an open standard that will also likely be available for a good long time. All modern word processors can read and write to it. ODF documents will be more easily edited, while PDF documents are harder to change and more likely to stay stable without unwanted edits in the future. Most scanners also support the PDF format natively and without any extra software. Scanning into ODF is much less common and, as such, harder to do without special software.

While most scanners can grab an image of the document and format it into a PDF that is easily stored online, they are less adept at getting the information out of the document. To do this, documents have to be scanned with OCR (optical character recognition) technology so that the text of the document is recognized and indexed. This makes searching for the documents later much easier, as all the text is available to be searched. With a traditional, image-based PDF, the text is an image without any context or metadata included (though sometimes the person scanning the documents can add it after the image is created). OCR generally works well with typewritten, clear documents. It does not work at all well with handwritten documents and transcription by a person may be necessary to pull the meaning out of the text. Even good OCR software, however, makes mistakes, so some cleaning up of the document might be necessary after the fact. Before you begin your scanning process, you will need to decide if you want to use OCR software to help pull text out of the document or if you want to use humans to transcribe and add metadata to the documents instead.

If you are scanning images to be stored, as opposed to text-based documents, one of the decisions you will need to make is the bit depth of the images you will scan. The bit depth refers to how many pixels are stored for each square inch of the image. Traditional preservation activities generally scan to a bit depth of 1200 ppi (pixels per inch) or more, ensuring that all the details of the original image are captured. It also ensures very large files, especially when saved in noncompressed image formats like .tiff. If your aim is access and storage as opposed to archival preservation, however, you can get away with much smaller bit depths of 300 ppi or even less. Most monitors can't display more than 100 ppi, though the retina display monitors available today can go up to 300 ppi. If these images are meant to be viewed exclusively on a screen and not printed out in any way, 300 ppi is fine. For printing, a ppi in the range of 300 to 600 is fine. Most basic scanners can scan in images up to 1200 ppi (though 600 ppi is more common), so any basic scanner will work for access-level scanning. Coming up with a standard bit depth that will work for your project will help keep staff and volunteers doing the work from having to make the decision repeatedly for different materials.

Scanning documents for storage can be a project in and of itself. The basic workflow is to collect the documents that need to be scanned, determine metadata (title and description at least), scan—adding metadata as needed or using OCR software to pull the text out of the document—and then take the newly created electronic documents and upload them to their new home in the cloud. This can be a big project for a small library, so the use of volunteers or other types of helpers can be beneficial. If more than one person is doing the work, though, the steps need to be documented in a detailed fashion—you want everyone working from the same instructions and doing the same steps every time. Some libraries, however, will decide that the work is too time-consuming for them to tackle and will decide to spend some money on a commercial scanning operation.

COMMERCIAL SCANNING OPTIONS

Commercial scanners can take your paper documents, scan them, and send both the paper and the electronic files back to you. While this takes some of the work out of the process for library staff or volunteers, it still requires that you collect, identify, and organize the documents to be scanned so that the company can scan them, then when you get them back, you still need to check them and add any necessary metadata to make them searchable in your storage container. Despite this, some libraries will find that it is cost-effective to have someone else do the actual scanning work for them, since commercial scanners often have high-speed machines that can do the work quite quickly in comparison to a traditional flatbed scanner available at most libraries.

The options for commercial scanning are many—there is usually a selection of such businesses in the general region of any library. Choosing a scanning company is beyond the scope of this book, but some general advice is to make sure the company is reputable and stable. There have been instances of companies going out of business, with the images they stored being lost or otherwise unavailable to the original owners. In one case, a company that went out of business had big problems with the items sent in to be scanned, "Some of the items entrusted to him now are in the hands of the receiver; some are with various investors; and some are unaccounted for" (http://www .maineantiquedigest.com/stories/a-negative-archive-deal/5133). While this is relatively rare, if it happens to you and you no longer have access to your documents, this could constitute a disaster all its own.

DO IT YOURSELF SCANNING (AKA PAPERLESS OFFICE TECHNIQUES)

Many libraries have paper records going back decades, at least. Those records have their own value as historical documents if nothing else! One way to make sure those records aren't lost if the building is lost is to scan them in as described in the "Scanning and Digitizing Documents Not 'Born Digital'" section in this chapter. Decide on how you want to scan them—as images or as text—and start on the process (giving yourself plenty of time and a few volunteers if you can swing it).

For current documents that you get in paper form, you can use a technique called the "Paperless Office" to help you get them into digital formats that can be safely stored in the cloud. The first thing to do is to reduce the amount of paper that you send and receive. Next you will want to have an easy-to-use and convenient scanning solution in place so that you can spend a couple of minutes a week scanning in the paper that has come to you and that you have had to produce for folks who haven't yet embraced the end of paper. Finally, you will have an office that can reap the benefits of having gone paperless.

To reduce the amount of paper you send and receive, there are a number of things you can do. First thing is to consider electronic faxing. If you are considering replacing your old fax machine, take a look at the faxing services that are available online. Those prevent other people from sending you paper—all their faxes are converted to electronic documents and sent to your inbox (fax or e-mail, depending on the service you use)—and they let you take documents that were born digital and send them via fax without ever having to create a paper version of them. Another way to avoid paper in the office is to learn to use electronic signatures. There are several options, from the not-very-secure image of your signature that you can add to documents to the much better option of using an electronic signing service such as Adobe's E-sign service or DocuSign service. Most of them charge a small amount, but the savings in storage and management of contracts can help offset that charge most of the time.

Having a scanner of some type near your office's computer workstation can make scanning in the paper received by mail or dropped off at your library a quick task. Many libraries have "all in one" type of business copiers which include copying and scanning in one machine. Some of the bigger ones also include a way to connect the machine to a file store on the local network or on the Internet. With a device like that, you can scan directly from the copier to the file server and make the process even easier. Once you have started the process of a daily or weekly scanning session (depending on how much paper you get), you will find that keeping track of invoices, payments, and other bits of paper that would normally be filed in filing cabinet is much easier. Using a file server—either locally that is backed up to the cloud or directly in the cloud itself—to store your daily documents and business records makes them both accessible by everyone in the office and searchable in ways with which paper documents just can't compete. Once the habit is set, scanning and filing your documents won't take much more time then filing does now.

So, once you have all those documents, both historical and current, put into a safe place online (or safe places, as recommended by the LOCKSS principle), you can start to see the benefits of keeping a paperless office. You will be able to get rid of filing cabinets as you empty them out, giving you more space in which to work and you will have easier time finding information as well. In a paper filing cabinet, a document can be filed in one place and one place only—and that one place really depends on the filing system of the person who originally put it away. In a digital filing system, the documents can be easily copied into a couple of relevant folders or found through a search of the server's file system so that the method of filing becomes completely irrelevant. Another benefit is that the information in your files will be accessible to you and to the staff of your library (as necessary, of course—you will want to keep personnel and other sensitive files in password protected folders) from anywhere they happen to be. That kind of accessibility can come in handy when staff are out of the office but need to look something up.

For documents that are born digital, the only thing you need to do is figure out where to put them. Local file servers are the traditional storage place for shared files on a network, but they waste a good amount of energy, processor capability, and hard disk space. Using a service like Amazon Web Services (AWS), you can have a server in the cloud that can be used as a file server with all the usual benefits of such as well as the benefits of being in the cloud. Other options include Dropbox, Box.net, and Google Drive as well as a number of other file storage options in the cloud.

The How Stuff Works site has a lengthy but comprehensive guide to creating a paperless office with tips much like the ones found here (but presumably they will be updated in ways this print book cannot) at http://money.howstuffworks.com/how-paperless-offices-work.htm. There is also a Wikipedia entry on the paperless office that contains some excellent references to resources you can use to help you on your way to a mostly paperless library at https://en.wikipedia.org/wiki/Paperless_office.

Chapter 3

Determining Needs and the Planning Process

Before you begin to plan where you want to go, you should be aware of where you are—knowing what work has already been done and what work needs to be done can be a useful input into the planning process. One way to make sure you know where you are is to do an environmental scan. This process just takes account of the current status of planning and disaster preparedness that exists and gives you a solid basis from which to continue your work. If you find that no work on disaster planning has ever been done in your organization, you can use this process to find out what other local organizations that are similar to yours have done and, perhaps, find good ideas that you can borrow.

An environmental scan, for our purposes, consists of a formal analysis of the state of the library's disaster plans. The disaster planning team can do this by collecting all of the policies, procedures, and supporting documents that the library already has and pulling out whatever nuggets of information or procedural instructions exist for disasters at the library. Once this is all collected together, the team can then determine what is out of date, what can be reused and what is not useful. From this analysis, the library can begin its planning process with a firm understanding of where it currently stands in the disaster planning process.

DETERMINING NEEDS—ENVIRONMENTAL SCAN

An environmental scan of your library and your situation is a necessary first step to any kind of planning. It's not possible to plan out a route to get somewhere if you don't know where you are to begin with! Once you know where you are in terms of what you are planning for (in this case, disaster recovery) you will be able to confidently find a way to get to where you want to be. Often environmental scans are used to find trends and directions in which the patrons of the library are heading so that the library can be there to meet them when they get there. In the case of a disaster plan, the environmental scan also includes a thorough review of where the library is and what kind of resources it has in order to be sure they are all managed by the plan.

Environmental scans for disaster planning begin with an overview of what kind of disaster plans you have in place to begin with. Most libraries have at least informal ideas of what to do in case of an emergency with their technology, even if it is just to call the local computer tech. Gather those kinds of plans and procedures first. Next, make sure you know exactly what equipment you have in your library. A list of computers, printers, and other peripherals, devices like tablets or e-readers, network hardware like routers and switches, and phones and fax machines, and all the other electronic equipment should be already put together for your Technology Plan, but if it isn't, this is the time to do it.

Next, take a look at your people. Who hold the positions that will be responsible for carrying out the disaster recovery procedures? Do they have the skills necessary? Gather their contact information and work schedules and get that compiled in one place. If they need training to do some of the things they will be expected to do, get that taken care of now. There won't be time after the disaster! Finally, consider the financial implications of a disaster. Do you have insurance? What does it cover, exactly? Will you have access to the information needed for your business office to continue operations in a new space if the building is destroyed? Is there a capital fund that will be used to replace damaged hardware? How much is in it?

GETTING STARTED

- Gather existing emergency plans
- Take an updated inventory of all computer / networked equipment
- Identify key staff (their contact information and their relevant skills)
- Identify backup locations and equipment should there be a disaster
- Clarify mission-critical software applications and data, plus financial options for replacement
- Identify and remedy potential key failure points

These questions should be answered at the beginning of your planning process and all the answers should be used to help plan the process. Most plans will start with your current environment and then move out from there, so a strategic plan outlining where you want to be in the future would be a good resource as well. Do you want to just replace what you had before or were you planning to make changes in the future that could be put into place after a disaster? Using the insurance money to make an upgrade to your network that you were already planning is one way to make lemonade out of the lemons of a disaster.

Part of the planning process is to identify the problem you are planning to remedy. This environmental scan will help you do that. By being aware of your current environment, with all its weaknesses and strengths, you can see the problems that are already in your organization and correct them. From finding single points of failure to recognizing a skill set deficit in your staff, problems that could affect your disaster recovery will start to become apparent after a good, thorough scan.

While you are doing your environmental scan, you should also look for single points of failure and try to remedy them before they fail. Single points of failure include a server in your building that, if brought down by a disaster, has no replacement either in the building or online in the cloud. They can also include a staff member who has all the technology expertise in your organization—do you have a backup tech in mind if the disaster affects that person? Pay special attention to the single points of access and the points of failure, which, if brought down, will affect the running of the library. Those things can be either mitigated immediately or, at the very least, considered extensively in your disaster recovery plan.

One part of environmental scanning—the analysis of the information gathered—is often given short shrift by libraries. There are a number of ways to analyze the results of the scan, but one of the most popular in the business world is by doing a SWOT (Strengths, Weaknesses, Opportunities, and Threats) analysis.

A SWOT analysis can be performed by spending a few hours with the planning team and discussing each of the elements of the analysis as it pertains to the disaster plan and your organization. You would identify the strengths of your organization and existing plan, the weaknesses in the existing plan, opportunities for the organization to change or grow while creating and implementing the plan and, finally, what threats exist that might keep the plan from being completed or fully implemented. Once each of these elements has been identified and discussed, the planning team can use the information created during this analysis to make sure that the disaster plan that is created is as strong and useful as possible.

THE PLANNING PROCESS

The planning process should be a collaborative and inclusive process as much as possible. There are several different types of planning processes from which your organization can choose, each with its own strengths and weaknesses. The defining characteristic of the one your library decides to use will be your staff—which one works in the way your staff is most comfortable?

Master Planning

A traditional form of planning is the Master Planning process. In this process, the plans originate from the administrative offices without much input into the plan from the people who work the frontlines of the organization. Master

Planning can use any (or none) of the formal planning processes listed below, but because this plan doesn't take advantage of frontline experience in the library, it can be less complete than a planning process that includes a range of people who work the desks or do other frontline staff jobs. This planning process is fairly common in the library world and is something that may get suggested at a "planning the plan" meeting—however, it is one of the least effective ways to plan for a disaster. Since this type of process doesn't take into account the expertise of people who do the frontline work, it is not recommended for disaster response planning, which requires those same frontline workers to make quick judgments.

Harvard Family Research Project

A more effective process is the Harvard Family Research Project (http://www .hfrp.org/publications-resources/browse-our-publications/strategic-plan ning-process-steps-in-developing-strategic-plans), which lays out a fairly traditional strategic planning process. It includes several steps:

- An environmental scan
- Vision and mission statement definition
- Goal setting and objective defining

It lays out a fairly traditional strategic planning process. This can easily be translated to a disaster planning process, with the vision and mission statement articulating the desired results of the planning process and the goals and objectives outlining the various systems and technologies that need to be protected and how that will be done. For libraries with extensive experience in various kinds of strategic planning (including technology planning, collection development planning, and so on), this can be a natural extension of just that kind of planning. You can use the same skill sets and processes that your library would use for any other kind of planning venture with this type of planning process.

Democratic Planning

The democratic planning process is another popular planning process in the library world. In this type of planning, each unit of the library would create a disaster plan that dealt with the issues and resources of that unit individually, with the "master" plan being comprised of each unit's individual plans. For example, the circulation, reference, and technical services departments might each create a plan that is specific to their department and that deals with the specialized needs of each department. The "master" plan then collects each of these (plus other departments' plans, such as maintenance, IT, children and teen, business office, etc.) and creates an organization-wide plan that takes into account the needs of each of the library's departments. In this planning process, the people who know the work the best and know what is most important for providing service to the patrons are doing the planning work. This is pretty much the complete opposite of the Master Planning model and can be far more effective, if managed correctly. Once each unit has its disaster plan, then a central planning committee or team can combine each unit's plan into a cohesive and complete disaster plan for the entire organization.

Project Management–Style Planning

Another planning process that is gaining traction in both the business and library worlds is project management–style planning. In this kind of planning, you treat the creation of the disaster plan itself as a project with several phases:

- Initiation phase
- Planning phase
- Execution phase
- Command and control phase
- Closing phase

For this kind of plan, you will create a project team—with a project manager in place—to do the planning for the plan, the plan itself and the final testing/acceptance of the plan. Having a project manager is crucial and giving that project manager the authority needed to create his or her own team and manage that team's work is essential. While getting the formal project management professional (PMP) certification can be useful for the person you choose to make your project manager, it can also be time-consuming and expensive. There are a number of classes, workshops, and books on the market now that will give your staff the tools and skills necessary to manage a project without the investment of thousands of dollars or years of work, as the PMP certification can require. Organizations like Library Juice Academy (http://www.libraryjuiceacademy.com) and ALA (http://www.alastore .ala.org/SearchResult.aspx?CategoryID=289) offer classes and workshops in project management topics and are a good place to start when looking to give your staff these skills.

Project management starts with the initiation phase, where you gather your team of planners (project team) and set the groundwork for the group to work. In the planning phase, you will plan by setting guidelines and boundaries for your process; this is the time to set the scope of the plan and to work out the details of what tasks will need to be completed before you start. The execution phase is the work of creating the plan itself, including work group meetings and the creation of plan documents. In the command and control phase, you monitor your planning process using the plan guidelines and boundaries created in the planning phase. It is important at this point to make sure you are staying within the agreed-upon scope and that you are hitting your target due dates for deliverables like your plan documents. Finally, the closing phase consists of a final review of the plan to make sure it covers everything you indicated in the planning phase, a meeting to go over the planning process you used and to determine what about that process worked and what didn't and, perhaps, a party to celebrate the end of the planning project. This is traditional project management and can be very useful to help keep staff working toward their goal of creating a disaster plan efficiently.

Project Managers

Any project management book or class can help you and your staff pick up some of the tips and tools that project managers use to successfully manage projects. One book that is specifically aimed to libraries is *Project Management for Libraries: A Practical Approach* (Buser, Massis, and Pollack, 2014). The organizations mentioned above—Library Juice Academy and ALA—are good choices for workshops or classes if those are better suited for your needs.

Many of the software and tools that are useful for project management are online and mostly free, or at least low cost. Software packages like Microsoft Project can be expensive and provide more overhead than you might need in a project like this. Some free or pay-by-the-month options that might fit a project of the size needed to create a disaster plan include:

Basecamp (monthly fee) at www.basecamphq.com

Asana (free) at http://www.asana.com—connects to other free services on the web to provide tools like Gantt charts that use the project plan and tasks that you enter in to your Asana account.

There are also Open Source options, such as dotProject (http://www.dotproject.net) that gives you the software to install on a server to use in-house. dotProject, in particular, provides all the functionality of Microsoft Office's Project software, though with a different interface. While it is free, it's also something that your IT staff will have to install with no guarantees of support. Other software and web-based services are released frequently, so a scan of the results of "project management software" query in your favorite web browser will give you the latest options for your planning needs.

True project managers spend years of their working lives and many thousands of dollars training and testing in order to get the PMP initials after their names. If you have a staff member who is interested and a number of upcoming projects that might benefit from an in-house PMP, you can support a staff member in taking the classes, getting the hours of experience needed, and taking the test. Most libraries, however, will find this both expensive and dangerous (a PMP can command a pretty high salary in the business world—you may find that after your staff member gets those initials after their name, they may be lured away to a higher-paying job shortly thereafter). For the purposes of a smallish project in a library, getting some training in project management without the investment in a full certification process can be enough. Many library organizations are now offering workshops and classes and preconference sessions on project management for libraries—taking advantage of those as they come up can be helpful for your library for more than just creating a disaster plan!

STRUCTURE OF THE PLANNING PROCESS

Planning is just determining—in advance—a course of action that will result in the achievement of a goal. The beginning of this chapter discussed the ways in which libraries can structure their planning teams; this section will concentrate on how to do the planning itself. The process by which you get there is relatively unimportant, though there are proven processes that have stood the test of time and which you should at least consider when setting up your planning process. In disaster recovery planning, you are looking for hazard identification and determining risk reduction in your plan. Whatever procedures you go through in order to identify those hazards and reduce those risks will be useful.

If you want to follow a traditional planning process, you can use a threefold method to get there. First you choose a destination. Once you have your environmental scan in place and know where you are, you can decide where you want to be. For most disaster recovery plans, that destination is twofold. You want to reduce the risk of experiencing a disaster, as much as possible, and you want to have a well-thought-out, tested, and workable plan to recover from an unavoidable disaster, whatever it may be. This is the part of the planning process that involves creating vision and goal statements such as the goal of having data backed up regularly, tested biannually, and recoverable within 15 minutes of a disaster or the goal of having a "hot-site" server in place that can be loaded with backup data and put into use within 20 minutes of the original server going out of service. Those kinds of goals are specific, measurable, attainable, realistic, and time based (SMART).

The second part of the process is to evaluate the methods for achieving your destination. These are the objectives that will get you to your goals. Rarely will there be a single way to make sure your goals are met—there may be several ways you could set up a backup service that helps protect your data from loss, but your job in this part of the planning process is to determine the best techniques to achieve that goal. Once you have identified the best way to set up, test, and deploy a backup procedure for your library, you can move on to the next goal in your plan and determine the best way to accomplish it.

Finally, once you've set up your goals and evaluated your methods of meeting them, you can decide the specific ways in which you will achieve those goals. In this part of the plan, you will consider resource allocation—who does what, what kind of budget they have to accomplish their task(s), and how much time they have to complete their duties. In the case of the backup service, you would identify a staff member (or role) who was responsible for backups, decide how much money the library will allocate to a backup service, and determine when that backup service should be operational.

Another way to approach the planning process is to use what is called Scenario or Contingency planning. This planning model requires you to consider any and all scenarios that might happen within the scope of your planning efforts. Once you have as many scenarios describing what may happen in the case of a disaster as you can get together, you can then start to use those scenarios to plan for them. In this model, you can choose to base your scenarios on each type of disaster (i.e., tornado, fire, flooding, hack attack, etc.) or you can base them on the results of a disaster (in a tornado, you may need to replace the whole building, but in a hacking attack, you may only have to replace equipment and not consider the details of replacing wiring or other nonconnected technology as you would if the building was damaged).

This kind of planning requires some creativity. You need to be able to envision what might happen in the future and come up with ways to either avoid those possibilities or deal with them effectively. Brainstorming is going to be a big part of this kind of planning and group meetings where everyone gets to give their input on what might happen in relation to their job will be important. One thing that you will want to keep in mind with this kind of planning, though, is that it is easy to forget whole sections of the organization if you don't have a checklist or master list to work from for every scenario you envision. One way to help mitigate this problem is to have a list of the major functions of your library (technical services/material processing, access services, reference services, public relations and human resources, business office services, administrative services, etc.) and make sure you consider how each one would be affected in each scenario so that you make sure you cover all your bases during planning time.

A third way to approach the planning process is to use a rational planning model to structure your planning. The general outline of this planning model is:

- Establish the problem—verify the problem exists, define it, and document it in detail
- Come up with all possible solutions to the problem
- Come up with criteria that show the problem has been solved (for later assessment of the quality of the solution)
- Choose the best solution you came up with
- Implement that solution
- Monitor the process to ensure the correct outcome and/or results
- Close out the process with feedback (using the assessment criteria generated above)

To successfully use something like the rational planning model, you will need to have an abundance of time and information—it won't work if you are so rushed that you don't get all the facts and nuances of your particular problem established at the outset. It also assumes that complete information is available. This isn't always the case, of course, when it comes to what will happen in the future. Finally, unlike the scenario planning model where considering the politics of each situation is a natural step, there is no consideration of politics and local circumstances naturally occurring in this model. Replacing a room or wing of the library funded by a prominent, and still present, local families might not be completely straightforward—especially if they contributed specific technologies or equipment as well. Changing things just because a disaster happened may be difficult in certain situations. You will need to keep those kinds of things in mind.

At the end of the planning process, when you have the problems laid out, solutions considered and chosen, and everything documented, then you can start to work on incorporating your plan into your organization. Add solutions that are to be implemented before disaster strikes to your library's procedures—make sure backups and monitoring of systems are done on a regular basis as a part of your library staff's daily/weekly/monthly duties. Update policy and procedure documents to reflect your new understanding of how to manage disasters and to incorporate your new methods of mitigating risks. Finally, make sure that the plan itself is kept in several safe places and that all of them are updated regularly and consistently.

As with most things in life, none of the planning options mentioned above are exclusive—you can combine some of the rational planning model with the traditional strategic-type planning ideas and use that hybrid to plan out your disaster recovery documents in your own way. As long as you are covering the basics, the method you choose (or the hybrid method you create) really doesn't matter—getting to the point of having a comprehensive and complete disaster plan is the point and however your library chooses to get there is fine!

CHECKLISTS AND BRAINSTORMING

Information on how to brainstorm is provided in Chapter 1 of this book, so in this section I will provide information on what to brainstorm. One of the best ways to make sure everyone is on the same page and all the disaster recovery efforts are being marshaled in the same direction is to come up with checklists for your plan. Checklists give your staff a concrete, step-by-step way to make sure everything in their part of the plan is done—and they are an easy way to take the fruits of your brainstorming sessions and make them concrete for future use.

As you sit down to begin your brainstorming session, you should make sure everyone is aware of the topic that is being considered. As was explained in Chapter 1, the suggestion to ensure that everyone knows the topic ahead of time is vital to get participants who are ready to come up with ideas. Once you have your group together and the brainstorming starts, try to write down ideas in action verb form. If, while listing the networking equipment that will need to be checked after a power outage, staff are just yelling out the names of the equipment, write down "check and verify lights on the router, check firewall lights, check and power cycle switches," etc. These will be elements of your checklist for the networking equipment portion of the plan.

The kinds of checklists you should be brainstorming to create will depend on your situation. If you have mostly outsourced major server technologies and have no servers in your building, you don't have to worry about checklists that deal with how to manage a server going down. What you might need to do instead is consider what steps (checks) you will need to do to ensure your connection to those outsourced server functions is stable. Each section of your plan should have at least one checklist that staff can use to help manage the tasks involved in making that part of the plan work for you before, during, and after a disaster. The sections below represent standard sections of a disaster plan.

INSTITUTIONAL INFORMATION

This section of the plan includes not only the name and contact information for the institution, but the list of personnel expected to carry out the plan and their contact information. You will want to make a list of everyone affected by the plan and get their information in one place to add to this section. This can also be a good place to put a checklist for making sure everyone in the organization is accounted for after a major disaster—if you have a list of current employees and their roles in the disaster plan, you can use that to make sure everyone got out of the building during a fire or after an earthquake.

PREVENTION

This part of the plan focuses on the kinds of things you can do to prevent a disaster in the first place. There is information about prevention services in this chapter and Chapter 6 and a discussion of the prevention section of the plan in the "Elements" section of Chapter 6. Refer to those to get started on brainstorming the kind of preventative measures your organization should take. As with most brainstorming advice, throw every idea into the mix at this point—you can go back and take out unworkable ideas later, but even "crazy" ideas can spark someone to think of something that will help you out later.

RESPONSE AND RECOVERY

Here you come up with response requirements and recovery instructions. The checklists you can create for this section can be highly detailed and work as step-by-step instructions for later staff to carry out during and after a disaster. Consider every aspect of your technological environment and how to respond to and recover from the loss of any and all of it. Once you've got a comprehensive list, put those instructions into checklist form and get them into your documentation. This will make the actual process of recovery so much easier when you can just go through the previously created checklist—one that was put together before the crisis—and make sure that everything that needs to be done is getting done. As each activity gets checked off your staff can move on to the next confidently.

SUPPLIES AND SERVICES

This part of the plan will list the supplies that should be on hand for a disaster and where they are located as well as the services that have been preselected for use in recovering from a disaster. Many resources that are listed in the back of this book have lists of common disaster supplies, so that part should be reasonably easy to compile. The services and service providers section may be more difficult. This is the time to evaluate and compare options from various recovery services and get them set up so that the staff don't have to make any decisions in the moment of crisis. Here is where you go through the evaluation process laid out in Chapter 5 for every cloud-based service you think you might need and list the winners of that process, along with account information and pre-disaster pricing information as a checklist of services to engage. Don't forget to recontact those companies to make sure they are still in business, still offer the same services at the same general prices, and that they are still willing and able to help you out in an emergency. Having an idea of what the prices are before a disaster occurs allows you to both budget for a disaster fund and makes sure that price gouging doesn't occur in the aftermath of a large disaster.

STAFF TRAINING

Checklists for this part of your plan will include skills needed to carry out the specifics of the plan as well as information that should be provided to new staff and through yearly (at least) trainings on the disaster plan for participating staff members. A good list to use for this section would be a list of topics that each person should be trained on, including:

- Where to find the plan
- Who is ultimately responsible for carrying out the plan
- A general overview of the plan
- A specific, step-by-step overview of each staff member's (or for larger libraries, each department's) area of interest in the plan
- Skills needed to carry out the plan:

  o In the backups section of the plan, skills relating to recovery of files
  o In the server section of the plan, skills relating to installing and configuring server operating systems and software

o In the computer resources section of the plan, skills relating to reconfiguring and installing desktop machines
o In the networking section of the plan, skills relating to configuration of routers, switches, and firewalls, along with the skills to set up networks in a new place, if necessary

While the actual skills needed to carry out parts of the plan are beyond the scope of a simple checklist, the list can make sure that all staff members attend the same training or have the same basic understanding of what needs to be done. It can be an overview of competencies, as opposed to a training document itself.

DISTRIBUTION AND TESTING

Finally, this checklist should include a way to monitor where the copies of the disaster plan are kept (locally and on the cloud) as well as lists of what needs to be tested on a weekly, monthly, and yearly basis. A checklist indicating where each copy of the plan is with a date that it was stored is something that will help keep far-flung copies of the disaster plan in sync with each other. Adding testing information—what needs to be tested in the plan and how often each element should be tested—is another way to make sure the plan doesn't get shoved into a drawer and forgotten.

All checklists will serve as a way to evaluate the plan and will give everyone a chance to work from the same page on how to interpret and deploy the plan, even if no one who was involved in the creation of the plan is around when it is carried out. The main thing to remember about checklists that you create for the plan is that they should be specific and measurable. Each checklist should cover a single point or section of the plan and should be specific enough to be used as a guide for those who will be implementing the plan.

WHO SHOULD BE INVOLVED

Putting together the team that will do the planning is important. You want to have enough people to have multiple points of view and multiple levels of experience, but not so many that the team meetings are impossible to manage. You also don't want to pull so many people into the meetings that the rest of the library suffers while they work!

There are several different ways to structure a disaster planning team. You can use one person from each department, ensuring that no one department is forgotten in the plan or you can choose people based on their planning and analytical expertise instead. You could create a small team of just a few people that each have an area of responsibility and let them create sub-teams of people to address those areas.

Another consideration is whether or not to bring in a facilitator or consultant from outside. There are many people who spend their working lives helping organizations plan and their expertise and experience can be both invaluable and expensive. Consultants can bring experience from working with many different kinds of organizations and can help keep meetings on track and productive. A facilitator can be helpful in this area too. Most librarians don't have the depth of planning experience a good consultant or facilitator has and, because of that, might miss big chunks of what needs to be considered in the plan.

Stakeholders, people who have a vested interest in the plan and its success, should be considered as well. Who are the stakeholders in your library? City or county officials might have a stake in your library, so they might be interested in joining your planning team. While including taxpayers—a large group of stakeholders—might be more than you want to do for an internal planning process, you may want to see if they have priorities of their own in disaster recovery via a survey or focus group meeting. They could help to set the priorities when other stakeholders and staff members disagree.

Whether you do it all in-house or hire someone to come in and help, keeping the team to a manageable size while making sure as many viewpoints as possible are represented is key. Consider carefully what the skills and strengths each member will bring to your team and only add people if they will contribute something substantial to your plan. Don't limit yourself, however, to just the people in your management team or your department heads. While they may have planning experience, other people in their departments may have skills that will be assets to your team. Consider schedules as well. Putting a part-time person on your team will limit the times you can meet, so that the person must bring lots of benefits to offset that disadvantage.

RESPONSIBILITIES TO YOUR COMMUNITY

Is your location a disaster relief area? Does that affect the plan? Some libraries are designated disaster relief shelters and some library staff are also disaster relief personnel for other agencies. Keeping this in mind is crucial for determining your actions, as well as who will carry them out, during a disaster. If your location is an official disaster relief station, you will not only have to consider recovering your systems in the case of a disaster but also dealing with people who are looking to you for help. If your staff have part-time jobs or volunteer with agencies that provide services during disasters, they may not be available to pitch in for your organization.

Many libraries are official warming and cooling stations for their communities and some are official shelters for their communities as well. This means that if there is a disaster, people will be coming to your building for supplies and shelter and you will have to deal with them besides any disaster-related problems you are having. Most libraries have emergency lights that come on when the power is out, but if you are providing shelter during a storm, you might need to consider having a generator as well.

A disaster plan can also help clarify weather closing procedures. If a major storm is headed your way, with potentials of power outages and long-term (longer than a day or so) closing of the library, having a disaster plan can inform your procedures for closing the library for an extended length of time. If the disaster gives you enough warning, you can shut down systems that could be damaged if the UPS (uninterruptible power supply) can't keep the system up long enough for someone to come back to it after the power goes out.

Your disaster plan can also help to identify "essential personnel" for your organization so that everyone knows who is required to work during blizzard conditions when only essential personnel are to be out on the roads. It can also make clear that your library doesn't have anyone who absolutely needs to be there to open and staff the building—if you are not a warming station or relief shelter, you may decide that your staff don't need to brave the weather to open the library when it is dangerous. Many of these decisions are made in libraries without a clear understanding of what the library's needs really are. Considering all this in a disaster plan will help make those decisions easier and more realistic.

Chapter 4

What to Backup and How Often

Backups are a necessity in today's world and many people are very good about making sure their backups are created and stored properly. Despite this fact, backups fail at a pretty high rate and recovery is often impossible for a multitude of reasons. Not only should your backups be done regularly, sent offsite, and stored securely, but they should be tested to ensure that they actually work properly periodically—at least twice a year, more often if you can schedule it. Backups also need to be done correctly.

- Backing up every file on every computer in the library is usually not necessary and can cause huge file sizes that are hard to store and hard to move out of the organization's servers.
- Backing up the wrong files can be both easy to do and difficult to detect for IT folks who don't do the jobs of most of the staff in the library and can't know what is (and is not) important to them.
- Backing up just the documents and files that are needed, without missing any but also without adding things like operating system (OS) files that can be easily replaced with an OS install disk, is the goal.

Unfortunately, there are no cloud-based tools that will make sure you are backing up the right stuff, and only the right stuff, for your organization. This determination will have to be made by the people who do the work in your library.

If everyone in the library saves all their work to the My Documents folder—and nowhere else—on their Windows machines, copying that is an easy way to make sure important documents aren't lost in a disaster. For organizations that use Windows domains, the user folders are a generally safe target for backups. Regardless of the workflow your organization chooses, each staff member should be involved in choosing the backup targets for their work machines.

Some of the shared administrative documents that you should be sure to backup include policies, procedures, and past reports. These are the kinds of documents that will be necessary as you begin operations again after a disaster.

Spreadsheets, including budgets and other financial documents, should be backed up as well. Another set of information that should be shared—judiciously—and backed up religiously is general passwords for the library's assets. No one person should be the gatekeeper to the library's passwords. They should be shared between at least the IT person and the director. Of course, the more people have access to them, the more often you have to change them when those staff members leave, but having more than one person responsible for and able to access the full range of library passwords ensures that if that person leaves abruptly, the library won't be scrambling for access to its own things. These passwords, however they are stored, should be backed up and protected vigilantly.

File and other servers are also important to back up regularly. Again, you want to avoid backing up OS files that are easily recovered with a fresh install of that OS, but you do want to make sure the files being served by the machine are all backed up properly. Each kind of file/web/application server will have different needs and different areas of the server to be backed up.

INTEGRATED LIBRARY SYSTEM SERVER

For the ILS (integrated library system) server, there are many bits of information that need to be backed up regularly. Most libraries employ a vendor to manage their ILS, but even if a vendor is managing the backups, the libraries should ensure that they know what information is being backed up regularly and that they have some say in what gets backed up. Library circulation data, patron records, item records, etc., are a must for backups because they will be necessary to rebuild a library during the recovery process. Knowing who has what checked out and what *should* be in the library when the disaster hit is essential for insurance purposes, too.

PURE FILE SERVERS

For pure file servers, servers that just store files that are shared among many different people, the important thing to backup is the shared folder that everyone has access to. If that server is doing nothing else, that is the only folder that will be needed. One thing that can help keep backups of a file server running smoothly is to clean it up occasionally. If there are historical files—stuff that has historical value but isn't being used on a regular basis—those can be archived somewhere else. This brings its own set of problems. Saving these files to a compact disc (CD) is easy and is one way to keep your backups small enough to be manageable, but CDs have a pretty limited effective life and you may need to move the files again when the CDs start to get old; also file formats change, so files saved in older formats might need to be saved again in newer formats on a regular basis.

WEB SERVERS

For web servers, the important parts to backup are the configuration files for the web software (Apache, MySQL, PHP, etc.) that you have altered along with the web content files. If there is a database used, as is often the case for websites using a content management system (CMS) like WordPress or Drupal, that database will need to be backed up properly as well. Again, the software for the database (except for any configuration files) won't necessarily be needed; that can be downloaded or reinstalled from installation media. The data files are what need to be grabbed and saved. These can be either the raw data files in the database folders or data dumps from a database client in .sql file format. The .sql files would be easier to import into a new database, but the raw files are easier to backup. Most databases have some kind of backup utility included—if you have one that saves all your databases as .sql format files, that is ideal, but even if you don't and you just get the raw data folders, recovery is possible (just harder and you may need to devote more time in your recovery plans to getting that done). Be sure to backup content folders in your CMS that runs your website, too—those will hold images, uploaded documents, and other information that will be needed to get the library's website restored quickly.

APPLICATION SERVERS

For application servers, the backups can get tricky. Many applications store their application folders and files in nonstandard places, like in user folders (generally the administrative user who has permissions to install software in a Windows machine) or in hidden folders in the C drive that starts with a period and can be difficult to find, but most use the "Program Files" folder on Windows or a /bin folder in Linux. Some applications give you the option of where to store the file and this should be an IT policy in your library, but be aware that not all software programs give you those options and documenting where each program stores its data can save time when setting up backups. It can be hard to figure out where applications put all their files, but if there is documentation for the application you are serving from your app servers, you can sometimes figure it out. If you are using off-the-shelf applications, the vendors can be helpful here, too. If you are sticking with open-source applications, sometimes a web search will turn up information on where application files are stored, but documentation can be thin on these kinds of programs, so it's likely going to require some searching. Once you've determined where all the important files are, make sure to add those locations to your backups. Don't forget to backup any applications needed for librarians to do their work—ILL software clients, files for cataloging utilities, and other specialized software is often time consuming to configure, so backing up the applications and their configuration files is important.

A note about installation media such as CDs that contain the installation files for a program—while you can usually get another copy from the vendor if necessary—it is possible (and generally advisable) to back up your installation media too. You can copy the contents of an installation CD to a folder on your cloud backup storage site and be assured that if the CD is lost or damaged in the disaster, all you need are fresh writable CDs and a CD burner to recreate the disk and reinstall the software. You only need to do this once—it doesn't have to be a scheduled thing, since the CD won't change! If you are using offsite storage for other paper/physical items, you could also do a burn of the installation media to a writable CD for storage there, too. Don't forget to back up your backup solution if you go with a commercial vendor—you'll need their software to recover your systems and if you don't have access to it, you might not have access to your files when you need them most! Keep a copy of the software you are using (or the scripts you have written) with your backups as well—it could be vital to your recovery.

MAKING BACKUPS

You have choices when it comes to backup solutions. You can do a home-grown solution using built-in backup options that come with nearly every OS or you can install a vendor's client to do backups. Every OS, desktop, or server, comes with a backup utility. It's not always the easiest thing to use, but it will work to make backups of your files. Once those backups are made, you need to store them somewhere outside your physical building. Backups do no good if they are destroyed in a tornado or fire, along with the servers and desktops being backed up. If you have multiple locations, you can send them off (through FTP or e-mail or the Linux rsync utility) to a location in another town for safekeeping.

If you don't have another location, you can purchase space in the cloud to store your backup data until it's needed. Most cloud storage providers can be pretty inexpensive—a single server can be backed up to the commercial CrashPlan Pro service (http://www.crashplanpro.com) for $10 a month with no limits on bandwidth used to move the files to the cloud or storage used once they are there. CrashPlan, along with the other commercial backup vendors like Mozy and Jungle Disk, have clients that you can install in the server to be backed up that automate the process, packaging them up, and sending them to the cloud. Many services also offer instant sync options, which give you the ability to create a "hot site" in the cloud that has up to the minute (or most likely five minutes) changes for every file so that if the server goes down only the last minute (or five) of work is ever lost. This is usually more expensive and vastly more bandwidth-intensive than the usual uploading of all the day's work to the cloud overnight. For mission-critical data and information, this could be worth the extra bandwidth and price, but many libraries choose not to spend their money on this kind of business-level backup solutions, finding that the costs of missing a few checkouts, and possibly losing those books is less than the cost of maintaining an up-to-the-minute backup of checkout and catalog data.

SETTING UP CLOUD BACKUPS

The usual process for setting up cloud backups goes something like this:

- Set up an account with a vendor.
- Download and install their client software.
- Open the software and go through the process of choosing folders/areas of the computer to backup (usually by checking a box next to the folders as they are listed in the client's interface).
- Choose a backup schedule (see the section on schedules just below).
- Close the client and rest easy until time to test (see the section on testing backups later in this chapter).

If you don't have a file server or a central location to store your files, you can still use something like Dropbox or Box.net to backup individual computers. Both services offer a relatively small storage area for free (as of this writing, Dropbox was offering 2 GB for free with their Basic plan) that you can use on any number of computers. Each computer in your library will need its own account, but once those are set up and a sync folder (such as the My Documents folder in Windows) is identified, anything stored in that folder will be immediately copied to the cloud. These Dropbox accounts can be shared, thereby sharing any and all documents that are saved to them to each computer either at the next sync (by default, that happens every five minutes) or when the computer gets turned on next and connects to the Internet. This is a great way to make sure all of your disaster plan committee members have access to the latest versions of planning documents, too. Just share a Dropbox account between the members and every time one updates a document, the rest will have access to it on their machines.

One thing I don't recommend is to use any solution that requires human beings to remember to do backups. People will fail—far more often than computers—at backing things up if it is left to them to remember. Backing up to tape, USB drive, or portable hard drive all require human intervention to work. This sort of thing is always problematic. You want to choose a backup solution that is as automatic and hands-off as possible—it will cut down on the possible points of failure and will make sure that fallible human memory isn't the reason important documents are lost in a disaster.

For those who want a homegrown solution using Linux rather than a commercial solution, *Admin Magazine* has an excellent article by Jeff Layton, "Incremental Backups on Linux," covering the details of backups using rsync, "Rsync is an administrator's best friend, and it can be a wonderful tool for doing all kinds of things that admins need to do" (Layton, 2015).   Layton gives a thorough explanation of how to do backups safely and correctly. His advice on how to correctly test those backups—"be sure you test the process, and be sure you create very good logs of the backup process—then check those logs after the backup" (Layton, 2015) is spot on and will save you countless hours of aggravation when something happens and you only then discover that your backups have been failing for a month. Pay special attention to the section on using SSH to secure your backups as they travel across the Internet if you are backing up any patron data at all and check the discussion about this and other security issues in Chapter 5 of this book. Layton talks about both full and incremental backups and how to manage them— including how to set them up so that users can access them to restore their own files, provided they have the Linux know-how to get them.

SCHEDULING BACKUPS

Backups are traditionally scheduled as full weekly backups with daily incremental backups happening overnight. What that gives you is a full backup every week of every file, whether it has been changed or not, with daily backups that are just of the files that were changed that day. This helps keep bandwidth needs down, since six of seven days you will have a pretty small file to send to the remote server as most of the changes that have happened to any data files will be relatively small edits or changes and few, if any, program or executable files will change at all over the course of a week. Daily backups should be scheduled every day, even on days when you aren't open, and they should be scheduled to run and be sent off to the remote server at times when you aren't open to avoid using up all your bandwidth for moving backups and leaving little for regular library use. For libraries that are open 24/7, backups should be scheduled at the least busy time when the chances of someone accessing one of the files and the bandwidth needs of the library are the lowest (in the wee hours of the morning, most often).

Most commercial vendors will have scheduling (as well as full/incremental backup options) built into their clients. All you need to do is set up the schedule (full backups on Saturday night, incremental backups the rest of the week, for example) in the client, and it will happen. If there is an option to get a report of backup actions in the client, take it. Even if you just glance quickly at it each day, it will give you a chance to fix errors or omissions in the backups before they become a problem. The report will also let you know if the whole backup was sent (Internet issues overnight could interrupt the transmission of the file and cause a backup effort to fail) or if the backups are getting so big that they are becoming hard to send in the window of time you've given them. For do-it-yourself backups, the Windows Scheduling Tool and the cron tool in Linux will be useful for you to schedule those backups to happen.

One thing to keep in mind if you have backups scheduled to happen overnight is that you need to be sure that all the computers involved in the backing up process are on. If you are backing up individual desktops at 3 A.M., but the users are turning off those computers when they leave at 5 P.M., no backups will ever get done! Servers are generally on all the time, so it's not a problem there, but for desktop and end user machines, you will need to either schedule the backups while the person is working (something that can seriously slow down the system and the Internet connection and is not generally suggested as a best practice for backups) or make sure that the computers are left on overnight.

TESTING BACKUPS

There is no point to doing backups if you don't test them, regularly. While many organizations do backups religiously, they still manage to fail a surprisingly high percentage of the time. Testing the backups can help find problems and fix them before a disaster (e.g., you get a virus that destroys the files on your machine and you really need those backups!).

The testing procedure is generally just a dry run to recover a file from the backup. You can identify a file that has been backed up and a date on which it should be recovered from and then go into your backup client to get it. Most of the time, you can navigate through a particular day's backups until you find the file, then download it to your local machine, and open it up to ensure it hasn't been corrupted or otherwise altered in the backup process as your test.

Sometimes, though, you'll want to do a full backup test where you do a fresh install of the OS and attempt to restore all the backed up files to a useable state. This should be done at least yearly, with the smaller test of just a few files at a time done on a monthly basis. However you choose to schedule this testing process, you do want to be sure you do it before a disaster hits. The worst time to be learning the interface for your backup recovery system is when you are also trying to recover a bunch of other systems from a disaster. Doing the testing will not only make sure your files are being backed up properly, but it will give you familiarity with the recovery process so that you don't have to worry about how you are doing it when a crisis hits.

Chapter 5

Preventing a Technology Disaster

Using appropriate cloud-based tools can be an excellent way to make sure your disaster recovery plan is going to work. Choosing those tools, however, can be difficult. There are a number of things to keep in mind when you are looking at cloud-based tools for any reason, not just for disaster recovery. Some general things to consider for any cloud service you evaluate are:

- *Bandwidth needs*—do you have the bandwidth to be able to make effective use of the service?
- *Pricing structure*—some services offer discounts for yearly payments, others are month-to-month only, with no yearly option at all—which will work for your particular budget situation?
- *Skill sets*—many cloud-based tools require skill sets that are extensively different than in-house tools—do you have those skills in-house? Can you get them?
- *Reliability of the service*—will it be around next year? Are current customers (and former customers) happy with the service? How stable is the organization running the service?
- *Scalability of the service*—even though you might only need a small storage space or just parts of a bigger service now, are there ways to scale to fit your needs in the future? Is it easy to add space or features to your service?

As you work through the different kinds of cloud-based tools, you will see what kinds of questions beyond these general ones above you will need to ask for that specific service As you work through the kinds of cloud-based tools you can use to prevent a disaster in the first place, you will see what kinds of questions you need to ask of any of your cloud-based vendors.

Prevention of a traditional disaster is not always possible. With technology disasters, however, it can be achievable—sometimes. This section will discuss ways to prevent a disaster from happening in the first place, as well as ways to manage your technology so that the results of a disaster don't have to be disastrous, though they still may be an annoyance.

SECURITY AND MONITORING

Two major considerations that need to be in mind when choosing a backup solution are the security of the files you are backing up and the monitoring system that will be in place to ensure backup problems are being noticed and fixed promptly. Any library that backs up patron data or documents that may contain patron data needs to consider the security of its backups both while in transit to the backup storage facility and while they are being stored as well.

The use of SSH security (Secure Shell—a secure replacement for telnet communications between computers) for homemade backup solutions is mentioned during the discussion of do-it-yourself rsync in Chapter 4 and is incredibly important to consider when doing your own backup solutions, but there are also considerations of security for commercial vendors as well. One of the first questions you should ask of any vendors is regarding their security policy—do they secure data being transferred and what steps do they take to ensure data security in their storage facilities? Their answers should show that they take customer data security seriously and that their data protections are at least as strong as the ones you use on the live data in your organization. Some very security conscious vendors will encrypt your data in the client at your location and only the encrypted data are moved and stored. This keeps the vendor's employees from being able to see the data, even when it is stored on their local machines. The only thing to worry about here is that encryption key—if the vendor doesn't have it and you lose it, the data might be gone forever, unable to be decrypted and used when it's needed.

Monitoring of the backup process is another way to ensure that everything is working as it should. The commercial vendors you use will generally offer an e-mailed log or some other monitoring system that allows you to easily tell when something has gone wrong on the backup. It's very easy for someone to make a small change and totally mess up the backups in process, with no one noticing it until the time comes to recover the backups that are no longer there! Even homemade solutions like the use of rsync covered in Chapter 4 can be monitored if you set them to log their actions and then make sure that log is viewed every day to make sure the actions taken were correct and complete. This should be a normal part of the IT staff's morning or evening routine—monitoring virus reports from the antivirus software (more on that in the next section) and keeping an eye on the previous day's backups.

RISK ASSESSMENT AND MANAGEMENT

One of the things you should think about when planning backups is risk assessment. Take note of the things (files, programs, data, etc.) that are vital to the operations of the library and that would be a huge risk to the library's day-to-day work if they are lost and make sure those things are properly backed up. The basic premise of a risk assessment is twofold:

- Figure out the probability that loss will occur.
- Estimate the magnitude of damage to the organization if it does.

One of the main uses of risk assessment is to determine both the probability of the risk happening and the severity of the consequences for your library if the risk happens. You can imagine a four-box chart with labels of high probability and low probability on the top and labels of high severity and low severity along the side. For things like data loss, the probability of loss is pretty high, but for most data files, the severity of the loss is fairly low—while they can and do get corrupted, many data files can be recreated with a minimal cost to the organization. For those items, however, where both the probability of loss and magnitude of that loss are both very high, such as patron or material data that are both important and expensive to replace—those are your targets for careful backing up and testing.

Another way to mitigate some of the risks of data loss is to be sure that the hardware you are using and the power going to it is backed up. The concept of keeping an extra machine around to use in case of catastrophic damage to hardware has been discussed already in this book, but along with that, you should also consider power backups as a way to help mitigate your risks of losing data. A good power surge—whether through a lightning strike or just a surge in the power lines—can destroy electrical equipment. Keeping a UPS (uninterruptible power supply) device between the hardware you want to protect and the wall outlet is a great way to keep that kind of damage from occurring. While a UPS and the batteries needed to keep it going aren't cheap, the old saying that an ounce of prevention is worth a pound of cure is definitely relevant here. The $500 or so you spend on a good UPS can protect you from having to replace many thousands of dollars of equipment.

When putting UPSs in place, don't forget about noncomputer equipment as well. At one library where I worked, the building next door got struck by a lightning and it put enough juice into our shared electrical lines that all of the switches we had in our network closet were fried. The insurance we carried covered the replacement, but the network was completely down for a long time while we got the replacements in and installed, so even though the financial hit was minimal, the "goodwill of our patrons" hit was pretty substantial (along with the "staff unable to do much work for a while" hit, too!). In a case where much of the library's infrastructure was in the cloud, this would have enabled the staff and patrons to access those resources, at least partially.

DETECTING

Another way to help prevent disasters is to keep the bad guys with viruses out of your systems in the first place. Information security and system monitoring should be built into your daily processes as a way to both protect your data and to guard against malicious attacks that can cause a disaster in your library. Many of the options that you have for both antivirus software and network monitoring services are at least partially cloud-based these days.

Antivirus Programs

There are many antivirus options on the market today—most of which are cloud-based in that you connect to the Internet to download new virus signature databases when they are updated. The way the general antivirus software works is that it contains a database of "signature" code that is known to be contained by various viruses and malware that attack computers. Every downloaded program and file that comes to your computer is checked to see if it contains any of the code associated with known bad programs. If it does, you'll get a notice telling you that the program or file has been quarantined and unable to run or be opened until you either confirm it's a false positive or delete the offending code from your computer—or, if you have strict IT policies in place, until an IT professional can come look at the program and determine if it's safe or not for you. If the code in the program or file doesn't match anything in the database, it will be allowed through and you can run or open it without any warnings—which is a problem if there is code in there that is so new it hasn't been added to the virus code database on your computer yet. This is why you need to update your virus software frequently (daily, sometimes) and make sure it's connecting to the Internet so that it gets the updates as they are made available by the antivirus software manufacturer.

One antivirus program that is available for consumer use that uses the cloud more natively and more completely than the standard antivirus program is Panda Antivirus found at http://www.pandasecurity.com/usa/homeusers/solutions/free-antivirus/. This is an antivirus software that is available for home or enterprise (network) use that keeps most of the information about virus signatures "in the cloud" for comparison against files and programs you are downloading. Instead of having a huge database of virus signatures on your local machine, the cloud is accessed whenever the software wants to compare downloaded code to known bad code. A much smaller database is kept locally for when there is no Internet connection. This puts the processing of the code in the cloud and helps to keep the bulk of the work from happening on your computer, which is a major cause of slowdowns from on-machine antivirus software. While Panda was the first to do this, the trend seems to be heading that way—many of the more traditional antivirus companies are using more cloud-based processing to help keep their customers' computers from slowing down whenever a file is being checked or an update is being downloaded and processed.

Another way that antivirus software is making use of cloud technologies—if not the cloud itself—is by creating a sort of private, limited cloud consisting of a "master" computer that each of the client computers running the antivirus software access—in the same way that computers access the cloud in the Panda software—to get updates and process downloaded files for malicious code. Eset, one such antivirus software vendor found at https://www .eset.com/us/, offers the Eset Cloud, which is a private cloud as described above, to give network administrators control over the antivirus software on many machines over a whole network. The "master" computer running Eset cloud can force updates and do other maintenance tasks without having to touch each individual computer on the network—it all happens through the private cloud set up between the master machine and the installed clients.

Whether you choose to use a fully cloud-based, private cloud-based, or completely non-cloud-based tool, the one thing you should always do is to have a way to be sure all clients are updated regularly and a way to be informed if any client starts to get out of date. While antivirus software isn't foolproof—sometimes the viruses come faster than the companies can push out updates—it is a huge help in keeping machines clean and keeping bad guys from destroying your data with a malicious bit of code.

Whatever antivirus solution you choose should be outlined in your disaster plan, along with a schedule for checking the updates and a person who is in charge of receiving the notices when the updates aren't occurring so that the problem can be fixed as soon as possible. Most commercial enterprise versions of antivirus software contain some kind of monitoring report that can be e-mailed out or at least a web page (local or cloud-based) that can be accessed to see how the clients are doing and what needs to be updated. They can also give you reports about what kinds of viruses have been detected and stopped and what kind of malware was caught before installation, which can be useful information for helping to justify the costs of these bits of prevention.

MONITORING

Monitoring your network is generally done from outside the network, which makes cloud technology a great tool to use. Monitoring of the network can include everything from scheduled "pings" that confirm that the network is up and responding to requests from the Internet to full-fledged, 24/7 digital eyes on your network making sure that the traffic is flowing and nothing out of the ordinary is happening. You can also choose to monitor individual machines, such as a web or application server, so that you are informed as soon as there is a problem with that machine—hopefully before anyone else notices it!

One thing to check, as well, is to see if your ISP or upstream Internet provider will do any monitoring for you. Some of them will, considering that your network health is important to keeping their network healthy, too. The kind of monitoring that a lot of ISPs will do is vulnerability testing—they will scan your network to make sure that all the known holes in the various ports and applications that you have are closed and so that no one can get into your network through a well-known hole or vulnerability. This protects both you and your ISP, since a virus on your network could affect others in the same area, so you should check to see if your ISP offers this service and, if it does, take advantage of it.

Some things to monitor for include:

- Uptime—make sure a computer is up and responding to requests
- Network response—make sure the hardware (routers, switches, etc.) are working properly
- Application response—make sure the applications on your network (local or cloud) are on and responding
- Vulnerability scan—make sure the known holes that bad guys can use to get into your network are closed
- Log monitoring—make sure you know what is going on in your servers by keeping a watch out for unusual events in your server logs
- Bandwidth monitoring—know how much traffic you have in and out of your network so you can keep up with traffic growth and not get surprised by big bandwidth spikes

The important part of a monitoring plan is that you do it consistently and constantly. If you don't know what is "normal" for your network and your computers, you won't be able to see a problem coming and head off before it becomes a disaster. You can use homegrown solutions, internal solutions, or cloud solutions—but any solution you choose should be implemented and watched so that nasty surprises can be stopped before they cause damage.

Whichever kind of monitoring you choose to do, there are cloud options to help you do it. In "20 Cloud Monitoring and Management Tools: Which Are the Best?" Talkin' Cloud® gives you 20 services that can do the job for you in different ways and at different price points (found online at http://talkincloud.com/cloud-computing-management/20-cloud-monitoring-and-management-tools-which-are-best).

CORRECTING

All the prevention and monitoring in the world won't stop every disaster. While some can be stopped before they happen with the right combination of backups and monitoring in place, some are going to happen no matter how vigilant you are. In that case, you will need to have a plan in place to recover from the disaster. With the right tools in place, you can make an unantici-pated disaster into a much smaller problem.

USING YOUR BACKUPS

After a disaster—whether it's a natural disaster that damages your entire building and all the equipment inside or a technological disaster that wipes out a computer's hard drive through a virus or a hard drive failure—you will rely on the backups you set up (discussed in Chapter 4) to keep that disaster to manageable proportions. Backups that are done properly and tested regu-larly can help your organization bounce back after a disaster without missing more than one or two beats—and can keep your very valuable information safe and allow you to start doing business again.

RECOVERY

The ideal recovery from backup involves loading your files, programs, and data into a computer (whether that's a replacement computer or a repaired one) and immediately getting back to work. Recovery should be possible for every situation from a single file that accidentally got deleted (a very common "disaster" in many libraries) to a complete system recovery with all the infor-mation from one computer being loaded into another for use. The recovery process will vary depending on your vendor (if you decided to go the home-grown backup solution route, see the following section), but for the most part, the idea behind the recovery process is the same—get the information from the backup file, load it onto a computer, run it, and be done.

HOMEGROWN SOLUTIONS

The recovery for a homegrown solution should be considered when creating the solution itself. If the backup is stored as a compressed file on another computer or in the cloud and, in your testing, you've been able to unpack that file and pull just the information you need from it (as well as all the information in the case of a complete system failure), you are probably ready for your next disaster to hit. This recovery process should be tested regularly and your backup person (whether IT or an assigned staff person) should be able to perform the steps required without having to think too hard about it.

That being said, you should still have those steps laid out very clearly in a worksheet or checklist so that if your assigned backup person isn't available to carry out the procedure, someone else can do it. Those checklists need to be tested as well, every time the backup is tested, the checklist should be checked to make sure the steps haven't changed and that the instructions work as out-lined in the checklist.

CLOUD BACKUPS OF SERVERS

Many of the backup solutions presented at the beginning of this chapter include backing up a server to the cloud using one of the available commercial vendors like Crashplan Pro found at https://www.crashplan.com/en-us/business/. While there are many other vendors out there that can do the job just as well and that might work better for your organization, I'll use the process as it works with Crashplan for this section. Most of the vendors will work the same way and this will give you a good idea of how the recovery process works without having to repeat it for several different vendors.

First thing to do after a disaster and after the computer(s) that have been affected have been identified is to determine what kind of recovery you need. If the computer that was affected is still accessible and only parts of the data on that machine were lost, you should try opening the Crashplan application, choose the "restore" option and restore the lost or corrupted data folders through that app—it takes you step-by-step through the process and makes things pretty easy. This is also the way you'd recover an accidentally deleted file, too—just open the application and find the file you need to restore, then ask the application to restore it.

If the server you need to recover is completely destroyed (physically or internally, such as a complete hard drive failure), then you have the option of logging into your Crashplan account on the web and restoring from there. Crashplan Pro has limits (250 MB per restore from the web at the time of this writing) that make it less easy and less convenient to do, so if you need to completely restore a computer from scratch, it may be worth it to install the OS and then install a fresh copy of the Crashplan application and do the restore as described above. If that isn't practical, however, the web restore option is available—just go to the restore menu in your account and choose the files/folders you want to restore. The files will download to your computer and then you can move them to the machine you need them in or just move them into the right spot if you are already on that machine.

CLOUD BACKUPS OF DESKTOPS

Desktop backups work in generally the same way as the server backups, but without the problem of recovering huge data files. Most of the time, if you use a simple cloud backup like Dropbox, the only thing you have to do is reinstall the Dropbox application on the new or rebuilt computer and the app takes care of syncing your files from the cloud to the new machine without any fuss at all. Other backup solutions might require you to download the files and put them where you want them, but generally they will all work in much the same way and unless you used a homegrown scripted solution, they mostly have applications that take care of the recovery for you.

One problem with the use of something like Dropbox is that if you delete a file on your computer, it's deleted from the server version as well. Dropbox, as well as other vendors like Box.net, however, keep a copy of your deleted files in the "trash" area of the website—you can just log into dropbox.com, go to the trashcan on your home page and recover any files you have accidentally deleted (in the last 30 days, at least, after that they are permanently deleted). The same thing goes with previous versions of a file—if you want to recover a previous version of a file that is less than 30 days old, you can do that from the website and it automatically syncs up and is delivered to your local computer.

CLOUD BACKUPS OF ILS

The integrated library system (ILS) is the core bit of software in most libraries—it includes all the inventory and customer relationship and financial acquisition information for a library in one place. Backing it up is critical and testing it is even more important. Most libraries have a vendor that supplies their ILS and those vendors generally provide backup support in some way. If yours does not, or if you don't know how to access your backups (if they do them somewhere other than your library, for hosted ILS options), it will be necessary to get that information from them in order to complete your disaster recovery plan.

For self-hosted ILS customers—where the computer that runs the software is in the building—doing backups regularly can be the library's responsibility. This means that if the computer that runs the ILS is damaged through a power surge, sprinklers going off in the event of a fire, or just a run-of-the-mill hard drive failure, the library's staff will be responsible for replacing both the server itself and the data that it held. Make sure that backups are being carried out and make sure that they are being transported somewhere safe (in the case of tape backups, still common in some ILSs). If the backups are happening online and in the cloud, something that more ILS vendors are offering, make sure your staff knows how to access the backup files and what is needed to replace them in order to get to the information quickly, in case of a complete failure of the ILS hardware.

For insurance purposes, at the very least, you will need to be able to list all the materials that were in the building when the disaster hit (if it took out the whole building or damaged it so badly that the materials inside were affected) in order to get reimbursed for replacements. Knowing who has your materials and how to get a hold of them in order to ensure they come back is also important, even if the ILS was the only thing affected by the disaster (in the case of a technology or hacking disaster). Many ILS software packages include acquisitions information that can let you know what's on order from whom so that you can cancel or redirect expected shipments. Most of the time, libraries are unable to get back to "business" as long as their ILS is out of commission, so making sure that backups are being done and tested on a regular basis and that your staff know how to get those backups and recover from them is critical for disaster recovery.

KEEPING OPERATIONALLY NECESSARY FILES SAFE

In Chapter 2, the section titled "Scanning and Digitizing Documents Not 'Born Digital'" covers how to scan in documents and keep them safe using cloud-based storage. You can review that section for specifics on scanning documents if you need a refresher. This section will discuss what sort of documents you should scan and how you should retain them for use in a disaster.

After a disaster, there will be a need for a bunch of documents that you might not use very often (insurance coverage letters, etc.) that you will want to be able to get your hands on quickly in order to start the recovery process as soon as possible. Some documentation—such as an inventory list with prices for all your materials—can usually be pulled from your ILS or other library management software, as long as those very important software packages are backed up properly, of course.

The best way to figure out what your library will need in the event of a disaster is to perform regular disaster drills. Just like you do a tornado or fire drill in school so often that when the real thing hits you know just what to do, you also need to drill the business office in how to recover from a disaster. If all the computers in the office are inaccessible—for whatever reason—and you are required to work from laptops in a nearby coffee shop, does the staff know where to go to get the documents required to get the library back in business? If your staff scans and files each business document (see below for a partial list of documents needed to recover from a disaster) and stores them in a shared cloud service (Dropbox, Box.net, Google Apps, etc.), you know they'll be available to you from wherever you have to set up shop after the event.

The kinds of documents that you will want to have available after a disaster include:

- Facility financial documents—leasing agreements or mortgage paperwork
- Facility plant documents—blueprints and wiring diagrams and other information about the facility itself
- Contracts for services for the building (landscaping, janitorial, maintenance, etc.) with contact information for contractors
- Financial accounts and account numbers
- Payroll and personnel information including contact information for every staff member
- Strategic, technology, and disaster recovery planning documents
- Insurance policy information—everything from agent contact info to coverage documents to receipts proving the premiums have been paid
- Receipts for items purchased within the last few years (5 to 10, depending on warranties and insurance replacement policies) for replacement purposes
- Any federal or state licensing or permit information, tax documentation, and other governmental receipts or proofs of payment

This is by no means a complete list of documentation your organization will need, but it will help get you started on brainstorming a list that is complete for your library and will be useful in your disaster plan as a list of documents and their locations for disaster recovery operations.

EVALUATING OUTSOURCED DISASTER RECOVERY SERVICES

Evaluating a cloud service is not very different than evaluating any other service you purchase for your library. You need to do some research to see what the available options are, what the general costs across the industry are, and what kinds of features each service provides. Once you have that research done, you can start to think about what your library needs from that service—what are the priority features your library needs in order to recover from a disaster with the least amount of time and fuss involved. After you have determined what the options are and what your needs are, then you can start to work through the available options in order to find the one that fits your particular needs.

When evaluating a service to determine its fitness for your needs, you will need to do both research into the service and as much hands-on testing of the service as you can. Most vendors will give you a trial period during which you can "kick the tires" and see what the processes are for using the service and for recovering from disasters with that service. While you might not be able to run a full test recovery within that trial period, you can do a dry run to see what the steps are to recover data and how easy (or difficult) that service makes it. For the research part, you definitely want to see what their other customers say—but don't just rely on lists of customers provided by the vendors, put some feelers out on various listservs and in meetings you attend to find other customers who might not be as happy with the service as the ones offered by the vendor. Finding real customers who don't have any reason not to tell you how it actually is can be very valuable.

When comparing prices between different companies, be sure you are comparing apples to apples. If the services are metered (you pay for how much data you store and how much bandwidth you use), make sure the comparisons are for the same kinds/types of data measurements. Most cloud vendors work in gigabytes these days, but if one of them is offering very cheap service in megabytes, you might want to do the math before comparing the prices.

There are a number of questions you should ask your vendors and coming up with a standard list (so that you are sure to be comparing responses to similar questions—again comparing apples to apples) before you start your evaluation process is important. The questions you ask will depend on what you've determined your needs to be and what kind of services you are looking for, but some sample questions you might want to consider are:

- What recovery time guarantees do you offer?
- What happens if a regional disaster hits? How do you prioritize customers?
- Are any hot sites you may set up for us industry-standard data centers? Can you offer us Tier III data availability/access?

- How do you test your services? How often do you test them? How do you involve our organization in the testing process?
- What kind of hardware and software will be provided at the hot sites you offer? Will it be compatible with our current environment?

Once you have the answers to these questions, you will be able to determine the service that will work for your library and your staff. Some of these questions might be more technical than your average librarian understands. In that case, you may need to call in someone who can help translate the various technical terms and specifications used for that service. For example, Tier III data availability is an industry standard used by data centers to indicate that they have redundant connections and *should* never have to encounter downtime in order to maintain or update the equipment inside. Definitions of the various Tiers can be found at https://journal.uptimeinstitute.com/explaining-uptime-institutes-tier-classification-system/.

CONCLUSION

While preventative measures are always a good idea, some disasters are completely unavoidable. The measures listed in this chapter, however, will give you some protection from a big disaster (backups) and might give you some warning that something is coming (monitoring). When you just can't avoid the disaster that comes, having a plan to recover your systems, data, and programs quickly and painlessly can make that disaster much less chaotic and difficult for your staff to deal with. Finally, evaluating the services that you choose for your disaster recovery toolkit requires careful research and attention to features and fit for your library. Choosing the right service can make all the difference when it comes to recovering from a big disaster.

Chapter 6

Creating a Disaster Plan

Disaster plans can vary wildly between libraries—some feel the need for binders full of information on what to do in a disaster, while others feel that a few pages of direction are enough for their organization. Whichever way you go (and there are downsides and upsides to both extremes), most plans will contain some standard elements in them. These elements are generally "best practices" for including in your organization's disaster plan, tested by organizations that have undergone disasters and know what was most helpful for them.

Below is a list of the elements found in a complete disaster plan and, in each section, a description of what would complete that section. Some of the elements may not be necessary for your organization, and many of the documents inside each element may be unnecessary as well. What I would suggest, however, is that even for a very minimal disaster plan, the organizational info and response and recovery sections should be included with as much information as you can gather, with the staff training and review/update sections added as procedures, if not as sections of the plan itself.

Remember that the disaster plan that is being discussed in this book is only a portion of a more complete business recovery plan that includes material preservation (for books and magazines) and human resources safety (which would cover what to keep on hand for humans stuck in a collapsed building, for example) along with many other elements. What is covered here is just the disaster recovery for IT functions part of a larger plan.

ELEMENTS

The elements of a plan listed in this section are neither requirements for a plan to be considered acceptable, nor are they the only elements your organization might need; they are a good starting point, however. The elements suggested in this section include Organizational Information, statements on the Scope and Goals of the plan, sections on both Prevention and, if that fails, on Response and Recovery, a list of Supplies and Services that will be needed during the recovery period, Staff Training aids for staff to learn how to use the document and, finally, a section that keeps track of Reviews, Updates, and the Distribution of the document itself.

ORGANIZATIONAL INFORMATION

To start things off, having a cover page with basic information about your organization is helpful here. In an emergency, you never know what you will forget—phone numbers that you've had memorized for years may be impossible for you to recall. In this element of the plan, you will enter all the information that might be needed about your organization should you not have access to your information technology after a disaster. Here you would put basic information about your organization—name, address, phone/fax numbers, etc.—to start things off. This will be useful if the worst happens and there is no one around who has all this information in their memory.

Next the plan should include information about staff. Just the staff needed to either make decisions about the plan's activities or carry those activities out, at least for this part of the plan. Administrative staff should be listed here, along with address, phone, and e-mail contact information, alongside their role at the library, and their role in the plan (whether that is just to approve certain actions during recovery or as a staff leader during the recovery process). Staff that will be carrying out the plan should be listed here too, with the same information available (name, address, phone, and e-mail contacts, role at the library and in the plan's activities). If your staff is large enough, alternative staff should be noted here if one of the main staff is unavailable during the disaster, for whatever reason. Your entire disaster planning team can also be represented in the staff section of the contact information of your plan, if they aren't already in the administration and "staff with jobs" sections.

Finally, include a listing of everything that your plan is protecting. For the technology section this means an inventory of your organization's technology assets. Include anything that needs to be replaced and is plugged into a wall:

- Phones
- Fax machines
- Computers
- Laptops
- Tablets/mobile devices
- Servers
- Printers/copiers/multifunction devices
- Scanners/receipt printers/RFID readers/etc.
- Security gates/demagnifiers

Google Voice Groups

There is a way to make sure that your contact information stays up-to-date and easy to use and that is by using the cloud voice service Google Voice.

You can sign up for a Google Voice account using a standard Google account and get a phone number that will ring several phones at once. One of the features of a Google Voice account is that you can pick up calls at any of your phones. That can be extended to a group of people as well—any call made to the central Google Voice phone number can ring all the phones for your group. Whoever picks up that emergency call will then be able to call that number again to get someone else in the group and so on. This can be a way to make sure that the information in the plan—the Google Voice number—stays current while you add and subtract phones from the account as people are added and leave the response team. While this would replace the need for the traditional "phone tree" in use in many libraries, you could still use that kind of document if your organization prefers—you just might want to store it in a cloud-based document service like Google Docs or Microsoft Cloud so that it's accessible from anywhere your staff might be after a disaster.

SCOPE AND GOALS

This is a brief statement of the scope (what the plan covers—and what it doesn't cover) and goals of the plan. The scope should indicate what the plan is intended to protect. If you are doing only a disaster plan that deals with your technology now, put that information in here so that if there is a different kind of disaster, the people looking for information will know not to look here. If you are doing a full business continuity plan with sections on disaster recovery and staff/patron safety and all of that, put that in this section. Whatever your plan intends to cover, make sure you give a brief statement of that intent here—and specifically list what it *doesn't* cover, too, if possible. Both statements are helpful when people are looking for information after the plans have been written.

As for goals—make sure you lay out your priorities in these goals. If you have a rare books room, make a goal to protect and preserve the resources stored in that room so that it's clear what you want saved and recovered. If your information is mostly digital and you want recovery staff to focus on that, make it a specific goal of the plan to recover as much digital information as possible.

This is a good place to put a map of the disaster recovery process for both small disasters and large. Here you can highlight the sections that will be useful for small, localized disasters and point recovery staff to the most important sections to consider for larger, more catastrophic disasters.

This statement does not have to be long. It can contain no more than:

This plan is intended to address recovery plans that affect collections, information technology and the facility. It does not cover issues of staff safety in general or of patron behavior (see staff manual for information on those topics). Human safety is most important here, no actions should be taken than might cause injury to people, regardless of the needs of the collection or technology. Plans to recover collections (you can list most important collections here) and technology (again, list most important tech targets to recover here) are implemented only after human safety is assured. This plan focuses on the most likely risks the library faces (list those here). Staff should be able to handle small emergencies like water damage or hardware failures alone using the procedures in the Response and Recovery section. For larger emergencies, see the Services and Supplies section for information on service providers that have been already identified for use along with staff.

That is enough to set the priorities and goals of the plan, lay out a scope of the plan, and point people to important information. You may find a slightly longer statement to be of benefit to your organization, with more detail added, but for many libraries, the above statement would be enough to start.

PREVENTION

This part of the plan details the steps you worked out in the last couple of chapters—what is done to prevent a disaster from ever happening. It's also useful as a procedures manual for staff for everyday use, not just for disaster recovery. Even if the worst happens, the information on what was done to try to prevent it will be useful in the recovery process. Start with identifying risks—what are the likely causes of disasters in your area, what disasters have happened in the past, etc.

The next section includes preventative maintenance—information on how, what, and where backups are done and stored, how often backups are checked, when virus scanning and other security checks are performed, etc. One way to organize this is by time period:

- *Daily*—backups, check virus software e-mail report, etc.
- *Weekly*—run scans on servers for virus/malware, check on emergency lights or flashlights in server room, etc.
- *Monthly or seasonally*—check window seals in fall to make sure leaks don't take out a server room, check that backups are working every four to six months, etc.
- *Biannually or annually*—hold drills for various emergencies, have inspections of fire suppression system, etc.

Knowing when you last did a drill or had an inspection done or checked on the backups is useful in many kinds of disasters.

Include the procedures for opening and closing in this section as well. If the procedures are documented here, the emergency responders should be able to tell what was done (what was locked up or unlocked, depending on the time the disaster happens, for example) and this could be helpful as they respond to the disaster. This is also useful to determine the state of the technology—if the procedures spell out how to open and close the library so that technology is protected in the case of an overnight disaster, this should be documented here.

Finally, include information about the facility itself. Have up-to-date floor plans and information about when maintenance was done on the building in the plan for use in the recovery efforts. Knowing where things should be and what kind of work was done on the building in the recent past can help staff access and salvage technology from the building. This is also the place to document what kinds of emergency shut-off systems you have for fire suppression or emergency alarms so staff know what to do to turn these systems off after the disaster.

RESPONSE AND RECOVERY

The response and recovery section is the meat of your disaster plan. This part should be widely available (distributed to every staff member, board member, and posted in strategic spots around town—the mayor's office, etc.—as well as online in several different places) so that it is easily at hand when a disaster hits, no matter what the disaster may be. There is some repetition of information, especially at the beginning, but you need to consider this section as a stand-alone document. It needs to be useful even if the rest of your plan is nowhere to be found. Even if the rest of your plan is there, most of the time, if the disaster is severe, the response and recovery team is going to go directly to this section and pay attention to it first (or at least they should, if they've been properly trained [see more in the training section later in this chapter]).

So, in this section, you can put the disaster response team you have put together (even if it's just the sole librarian and a board member—however big or small your team is, list them here) so that if the folks recovering from the disaster are working with only this section, they have the necessary information to get in contact with the members of the team. You can also reproduce the hardware and software inventories here as well.

Other information that you'll want to have in this section is software reconfiguration instructions, relocation information, and information about alternate forms of communication and operations in the event of a catastrophic disaster. Your software reconfiguration instructions should include details about how each mission-critical piece of software in your library (ILS, Quickbooks, etc.) is configured. A copy of the config file, if available, is useful here. Instructions on how to make sure the software works properly— tricks to installing it in a new environment, if necessary, and that sort of thing—are useful as well. Pointers to data backups would be handy here, too—you don't have to recreate all the information about your backups here, though, just where you put them and how to access them would be sufficient. The relocation information should include potential sites where your business operations can be set up. City or county offices might offer some shelter for your administrative staff, or you might contract with a co-working space or other shared office areas in your town to use them if necessary. Make sure any potential relocation areas are sufficiently connected to the Internet. Finally, having information about your telecommunication services—Internet and phone especially—so that those services can be turned back on (or ported) to your temporary location is useful to have here too. This will help get phone lines back in place and put your library back in touch with the outside world.

Beyond the IT considerations, you should also be including real-world information about what your priorities are for saving physical items like hardware, furniture, collection materials, and, most importantly, list out the rare and hard-to-replace items that you need to try to save first. Insurance information would also be useful here—at least the information for your local agent, but a general overview of what is covered and what sort of information you need for claims would be helpful here. Finally, include evacuation and emergency procedures in this section. Make sure your staff know the material here, too—they should be well trained with drills on how to respond to an emergency and how to evacuate themselves and your patrons quickly and safely.

SUPPLIES AND SERVICES

Here is where you list the companies that you've already vetted for use after an emergency. (See Chapter 3 for information on finding, vetting, and keeping in contact with emergency services companies in the "Supplies and Services" section of the planning process.) Have contact information, lists of services, and prices for each of the services you might use. If you have found, vetted, and decided on a particular IT company to help you in the process of recovering from a disaster, it gets listed here with all the information necessary to find and engage its help when all else may be lost. You should also have emergency contacts at fire and police stations as well as at hospitals in the area. Those contacts should be familiar with the library (they should visit at least yearly to keep up that familiarity) and should be aware of the kinds of services your organization would need from them in an emergency.

For supplies, this will mostly be for physical items (survival supplies for staff and patrons caught in the building for an extended period of time, tarps and things that will be useful in many ways during many different types of disasters, etc.) but you should think of your needs in the IT arena as well. Consider where extra cables will be sourced from and what vendors close to you carry the kinds of replacement hardware needed to quickly recover a server or desktop machine from a localized disaster (virus wiping out the hard drive, RAM or other sensitive equipment getting destroyed in a power surge, etc.).

This is also a good section to put your emergency funds information, so that recovery staff know how to access funds with which to purchase those emergency supplies. Other information that can go here are emergency personnel—volunteers and others who can be called on to help in an emergency, consultants that can be used to help get your IT operations back up (perhaps for less of an emergency than the IT company you listed above under emergency services, but more than your current staff can handle alone) and anyone else who might be useful in an emergency situation.

STAFF TRAINING

Training is vital and, if possible, should be documented in the plan itself. There are several targets for disaster plan training, starting with the planning team, continuing on to the recovery team, and finishing with the general staff training. For the planning team, training on what needs to be done to create a proper disaster plan is useful for updates and revisions—this is training on the process of creating the plan itself and can give guidance for future updates to the plan. For the recovery team, the training should use the plan as written to inform the training, perhaps by creating a training document that provides an index to the parts that the recovery team would find most useful—the recovery team should be very familiar with the plan and should also be trained on any skills needed to carry out the plan (recovering backups or replacing computers, for example). Staff training should be done as well, though it can be far more general than the recovery team's training. I would suggest that the recovery team actually do the training for the staff (nothing helps you learn new information than having to teach it to someone else) to get them familiar with the plan and the procedures that are kept within. Staff training should also include emergency response—where to evacuate patrons, when to call a member of the disaster team in to determine if an emergency has happened, and who to contact in case of various kinds of emergencies or disasters.

You can also use this part of the plan to indicate if general CPR or first aid training is necessary for staff, as well as other kinds of outside training (technology-related, generally) that might be advised by the planning committee or group. Most organizations will need to increase staff skills in technology to carry out the recovery part of the response and recovery process, and identifying what training is available to give staff those skills can be done here.

FROM DISTRIBUTING TO UPDATING

Distributing the plan widely is the best practice. You should have copies in administrator's homes, in far-flung branches or collaborative libraries (ones where you have made an agreement to store these plans in case of a general area-wide catastrophe), and online in more than one place. You may want to make sure each member of the management team or the board has a copy as well.

The plan needs to be reviewed at least yearly. Every six months would be ideal, but may be impractical depending on how big the plan is in comparison with your staff. Every year is pretty much the longest you should go without reading through the plan with an eye for changes in policies, procedures, or technology landscapes. The tech inventory should be updated yearly as well, during this review process and that updated inventory should be included with your lists of general inventory for insurance purposes, too. This is the time to make sure that the procedures laid out in the plan are still being followed and that the testing of the plan (as indicated in the plan itself) is being done.

The plan should be fully updated every three to five years. If the yearly reviews have been happening, this will be a much shorter process than the original writing of the plan. This goes a bit deeper than a review in that you are not only checking to make sure the plan's procedures are being followed but that they still make sense and are still necessary in your current environment. You also will want to look for things that have changed that you can either eliminate or add to the plan to make sure you are fully protected. Some of this stuff will be handled during the reviews, much of the deeper thinking might not be, however.

TEMPLATES

There are a number of places on the Internet where you can get good templates for a disaster plan. Some of the best are noted at the end of this section, but the Internet is a fast moving thing and sites change and move between being written about and being read about. That being said, there are some places that you can go that will likely always have some information for you if the templates listed below all go away in some future iteration of their sites.

One of the most stable sites is the dPlan site. This is a free service that leads you through the process of creating a disaster plan by having you fill in a form on the web and then printing the resulting plan. There is a lite version that is suitable for smaller organizations and the full version that will work for larger libraries. This site has been around for a while and appears that it will be around for a while longer.

Most of the "collections of templates" sites that I found were full of dead links and missing information. If this happens to you as you are looking for the information in this book, a Google search on "Disaster recovery templates" will give you a huge number of templates to choose from. Use the information contained in the rest of this book to help you find a template that is complete and easy for you to use.

DISASTER RECOVERY TEMPLATES

ALA Disaster Preparedness and Recovery—http://www.ala.org/advocacy/govinfo/disasterpreparedness

Baltimore Academic Libraries Consortium Disaster Preparedness Plan—http://resources.conservation-us.org/disaster/baltimore-academic-libraries-consortium-disaster-preparedness-plan/ (Sections C and D discuss electronic and technical disaster preparedness)

CoOL Disaster Plan Samples—http://cool.conservation-us.org/bytopic/disasters/plans/

Cullman County Public Library System—http://www.ccpls.com/press/CCPLS%20Disaster%20Manual_edit.pdf (post disaster process on page 9)

dPlan—http://www.dplan.org

MS Word Disaster Recovery Plan Template—http://blogs.technet.com/b/mspfe/archive/2012/03/08/a_2d00_microsoft_2d00_word_2d00_document_2d00_template_2d00_for_2d00_disaster_2d00_recovery_2d00_planning.aspx

New York University Library Disaster Planning Workbook—http://www.ccpls.com/press/HURRICANE%20PLAN%20FOR%20ORANGE%20BEACH%20PUBLIC%20LIBRARY.pdf

Orange Beach Public Library Hurricane Preparedness Plan—http://www.ccpls.com/press/HURRICANE%20PLAN%20FOR%20ORANGE%20BEACH%20PUBLIC%20LIBRARY.pdf

South Central Regional Library Council's Disaster Plan—http://scrlc.libguides.com/loader.php?type=d&id=342404

TechTarget Disaster Recovery Plan Template (Word format)—http://cdn.ttgtmedia.com/searchDisasterRecovery/downloads/SearchDisasterRecovery_Network_Disaster_Recovery_Plan.doc

APPENDICES AND SUPPLEMENTARY INFORMATION

Many of the sample plans and templates listed in the box above include much of the information needed in a disaster in appendices to the main document. This is fine, if you choose to do it this way, but do be sure that the information is clearly marked in the Table of Contents and referred to in the relevant sections. The last thing you want is for staff, during an emergency, to be flipping around in the plan looking for specific information and to be unable to find it.

Some of the things you can put in your appendices include a list of contacts, either separate from or copied from the list of contacts in the introduction material of the plan, library floor plans, a general inventory of items to be checked after the disaster, and any necessary forms required for recovery purposes (purchase order forms, insurance claim forms, etc.).

Chapter 7

What Is a Successful Disaster Plan?

So, you've gone through the disaster planning process, you have a plan and you are ready to put the whole thing behind you, right? Not so fast. Once your plan is in place, you can be sure it is useful and successful only if you test it. Testing it immediately gives you some quick feedback to fine-tune the plan and testing it periodically thereafter gives you information about what's changed in your environment that might not yet have made it into your plan.

One thing that you will need to do is to budget for testing. Some tests can be done relatively inexpensively, using only staff time, but more involved and accurate testing might need to recreate a full shutdown of your library's IT to make sure that the failover or hot site plan you have in place will work. That will require either paying for IT staff to come in over a holiday or closing the library for a day while your systems are being repeatedly rebooted during the tests. Every plan will require some investment of resources, so this should be built into the library's budget every year.

Once you've done the testing, what does "success" look like? Generally, it will mean that you have confirmed that the directions and procedures you have in your plan work under conditions very similar to that of a disaster. Not all disaster plans (such as the ones that involve spraying water from the ceiling in your server room to put out a fire) are going to be feasible to be tested exactly. Sometimes you will have to fudge the situation to just get close, but if you do that and things go smoothly and systems are brought back online quickly and everyone knows what they are supposed to do, well, then you have a test that is a success.

TESTING THE PLAN WITHOUT CAUSING A DISASTER

One part of testing that will come in handy when revising that should be incorporated into every type of test you do is to create a "lessons learned" section in the testing documentation. Whether it's a small comment section at the bottom of a testing checklist or a full-blown report at the end of the total systems test, it will be useful when going back through the plan later to update it based on what you learned. This section of the testing plan should be in place before testing happens and staff who do the testing need to pay careful attention to what they are learning from the testing and document it as the learning happens. Going back later and trying to remember what you learned after the fact will be far less useful than writing it down when it's fresh.

The structure of the lessons learned section should include a brief note on what was tested, how the test went, and a free-form area for comments from the tester. The kinds of things that the tester is looking for are:

- Deviations from written procedure (for whatever reason)
- Changes in file or application locations
- Quirks of the recovery process
- Unusual results that need follow-up

The tester should record all the data they collect from their testing and make sure they are in place so that revising the plan can be done relatively painlessly.

TESTING STRUCTURE

Deciding on the test structure will be your first order of business. You can start by determining the frequency of each type of test that follows in this section (checklists, walkthroughs, individual components, whole systems, entire plan). The first types of tests, the ones done mostly on paper and in your imagination, can be done fairly frequently without a huge strain on the organization. Going through a checklist every six months to a year is reasonable to ensure the checklist is up-to-date and everyone who needs it is familiar with the lists. Walkthroughs can be done reasonably frequently as well, as those won't necessarily affect the operations of the library. Beyond that the individual systems might only need to be done yearly or every two years and the whole system/full plan tests might only need to be done every two to three years (or at least once during the life of the plan). Those last kinds of tests will require operationally necessary systems to be shut down in order to test the process of bringing them back up. This may need to happen several times to test responses to several different disaster scenarios (a fire disaster will require a different response than a "human error erased everything on the hard drive" sort of disaster).

CHECKLIST TESTING

Checklist testing is just going through the checklists and making sure they make sense, cover the basics of what needs to be done, and are complete as written. Have someone with some domain knowledge do this kind of testing for your organization. If you are going through a checklist on how to recover from backup, have the IT person (or team) responsible for backups doing the testing of that checklist to determine if it makes sense from their experience and perspective. They can also help to be sure that the checklists cover the basics of what needs to be done. The next step of walkthrough testing will have nonexperts in the room as well to help make sure the instructions are clear even for non-IT people, so that's not a concern for right now. Finally, make sure the checklists are complete. Missed steps and forgotten processes will just cause problems during a stressful recovery, this is the time to make sure everything that needs to be in the list is there and it makes sense to any user.

The process of checklist testing is pretty straightforward. You choose a checklist (or a few) to test and you make copies of it (or them) for the individual (or two, at most) who has been given responsibility for this area of the plan. Starting at the top, with the explanation of the checklist, that individual will go through each section and consider each and every step listed on the page. This will require some imagination, at times, as the person will have to remember how to do things without actually doing them, which can be challenging. Encourage the testing staff member to imagine, step-by-step, the process that you are checking so that the possibility of missing a step is reduced.

At the end of the test, after you have gone through the steps and confirmed that they are all there, complete, and reasonable, you can sign off on the checklist as "tested." This should be done fairly frequently, as processes change and details may be different for new processes. You can also use this type of testing for non-checklist portions of the plan—just read through the various sections to make sure they contain the information they should and are clear enough to be understood during a stressful time. The thing to remember here is that you aren't going to be touching any hardware or messing with any software—this is all a mental exercise that is going to be doable without taking down or otherwise altering any operational systems.

WALK THROUGH TESTING

This is very similar to the checklist/paper testing above, but with a group of people and it will test multiple areas of the plan at once. This can be structured in different ways, too. You can convene a group of people to "walk through" a particular disaster or you can get an entire department together to "walk through" their responses to different kinds of disasters. The idea in this kind of testing is to work through the process in a group, without actually performing any of the steps of the plan. One thing to remember, though, is that you want both experts and nonexperts in these groups. The only way to make sure the plan is written clearly enough that it can be followed easily in an emergency is to make sure that people who have no experience with, for example, backups, are included in the walkthrough tests of the backup plans.

In the first kind of walkthrough test, you can get your disaster recovery response team together, let them know what kind of disaster just befell the library, and start working through the steps each person should take, based on the instructions in the plan. Doing a complete walk through of an entire disaster will help you spot weak areas or just plain missed areas of the plan that can be bolstered before an actual disaster hits.

Likewise, for a departmental test, you can gather the members of the department together to discuss how they need to respond to each kind of disaster that is laid out in your plan. This helps the staff know what to expect in case of a disaster and, again, gives you some insight into weak or nonexistent areas of your plan that are hard to find without this kind of thorough test. This also makes sure that everyone has at least read through the plan and has at least a basic familiarity with what it says.

Some of the things that should be looked at in particular during this kind of test include contact lists and call trees, vendor information, and closing procedures for the library itself or for particular parts of the library (shutting off an area that is flooding, for example). You can review other parts of the plans, of course, but the really helpful (and easier to get people's heads around) parts are the less technical parts of the plan.

Contact lists and call trees should be reviewed for completeness and to make sure the staff being contacted are up-to-date—new staff added, former staff removed. If you are using something like Google Voice, you should log into the account occasionally to check that phone numbers are still correct and try calling the Voice number to make sure everyone actually gets the call. Vendor information should be reviewed here too, especially during departmental walk-throughs, since most departments can verify vendors they work with regularly at a glance. Closing procedures are important just to make sure that everyone has read through them and understands what needs to be done to make sure the building is closed and secured in case of a disaster. Familiarity with these procedures will make a big difference in how well they are carried out under pressure.

TABLETOP OR SIMULATION TESTING

This kind of testing is sort of like running a drill. A disaster scenario is thrown at your staff (during all-staff meetings or staff development days, preferably—some time when patrons aren't around to distract!) and they have to respond accordingly. This is like the walk through test in that actual systems aren't touched, but it's a bit more involved with some role-playing elements. Just like in a fire drill, the administrator can come into a meeting of staff and announce the disaster has occurred. This is a good way to try out different scenarios, too. What if the IT manager is in Tahiti and completely unreachable—who is the second in command of the department, who knows what that person knows, and can perform those duties in their absence? You can also test specific disasters here. What if a car runs into the building and takes a big chunk of the north wall? (The number of cars that have run into library buildings between writing about that being a type of disaster to be aware of early in the book and now is really astonishing—it happens a lot!) Do you know where the library's electrical plans are? Do you know what systems have been affected by the wiring on that wall becoming nonfunctional? Do you know how to evacuate patrons from the rest of the building while also keeping other patrons out of the affected areas?

TECHNICAL PARTS TESTING

Here is where you finally get to put your hands on your various library systems and check to see if they will work as expected in an emergency. You can start by testing the UPS systems to make sure they keep the computers running long enough to do proper shutdowns (in case of an electrical outage). You can do this with spare UPS and server machines to keep the disruption to the library at a minimum. Continue the tests by checking backup recovery processes—backup a folder, some files, an entire server's worth of data—by recovering those backups to a third location. Having a spare portable hard drive is handy here, but any location that will neither overwrite the current information nor overfill a storage area is fine. This is parallel testing and is the safest and least disruptive way to test your systems.

Live testing involves actually taking down a system to see what your staff do, how the plan works, and what needs to be tweaked in order to make it work during a real disaster. This will require you to actually shut down systems that may be required for normal library operations, so you may want to schedule these tests after hours, on staff development/training days, or during times when you can bring the library's systems down for a brief period of time (slow times, scheduled upgrade times, etc.). You can take down the library's integrated library system (ILS) during this test to practice what staff should do in the case of a loss of data or access to that system. If you have offline circulation procedures, this is the time to make sure the staff understand and can perform those procedures. You can also shut off all electrical and Internet access to the building to make sure everyone knows what to do in those situations. You can run full-scale fire, tornado (or hurricane), and earthquake drills along with the first responders who will be working alongside your staff in these situations. Fire and police departments will generally be more than happy to help out here—the more they know about your situation and your building, the safer they will be when responding to a call, so they have some motivation to join you!

FULL-SCALE TESTING

This kind of testing is both expensive and time consuming, so it won't be done very often, but it should be done at least once during a plan's life. For full-scale testing, you actually switch your services to your hot site (if you have one set up) or you imagine that all has been lost and you start recovering from backups and extra machines. Here you start with the premise that you've lost everything and you need to restart library services from what you have saved in backups, stored elsewhere in terms of extra/backup hardware, and contracted for with your vendors.

This is where having an Amazon or Google or Microsoft cloud account comes into play. You can take the backups that you have and recreate as much of your library's technological infrastructure as possible on their cloud-based hardware. Test to make sure you have everything you need being backed up at this time. Test also to make sure that you have the skills on hand, or contracted through a vendor, to be able to recreate and connect to your library's infrastructure from where ever your second site may be (in the case of a complete loss of your main building, for example).

This is the time to work on restoration of media (or cloud) backups. You should test both targeted backups and full-scale server restore backups. Often things have to be installed in a particular order (OS first, applications second, data third) so knowing that and having it clearly spelled out in the plan is a benefit to those who will be doing this under pressure later.

This is also a good time to work on priorities and make sure they are clearly laid out in your plan. If you have particular collections or particular hardware that must be saved before anything else, this is the time to make sure that is spelled out clearly in the plan. Often it will be more important to get rare and expensive books and materials out of the library or at least up off the floor or away from water in general than it will be to make sure the server (which is a commodity item—the important stuff is in the backup which, hopefully, is offsite and not at risk) is protected and saved. You will want to be sure to practice preservation steps for the collection as well as for your data during this test.

Sometimes this kind of test actually can be done without interfering in day-to-day operations of the library, since it assumes that the library no longer exists, so it's something that can be scheduled during regular library hours. It will require activating various staff members and paying contractors and vendors for their time during this test and it will require paying for the cloud resources you use to recreate your infrastructure online, but it will be worth it to know that your plan is able to cope with the worst of disasters and that your library will continue to function as an organization, even if the building is gone.

DOCUMENT THE TEST PLAN

You should include the testing plan in the disaster plan. It should be clear how you intend to do the testing, when you intend to do the testing, and how often each part of the plan will be tested. You should include, in this part of your plan, who needs to be notified if you are doing various tests such as the library's board or the first responders in your area (if you work with an ILS vendor and will be testing it, make sure your vendor is aware—they might have tips for you!). You should also include the results of the tests in your plan. Those results may be helpful for the staff who are carrying out the plan in a real disaster.

SAMPLES FOR SMALL LIBRARIES

For small libraries, a simple declaration of priorities (including those of the humans involved over the technology), a list of likely disasters, and steps to take in the case of small- and large-scale disasters would constitute a perfectly acceptable disaster plan. The sample below could be the entirety of the plan, with an appendix (or two) with the staff contact, vendor/consultant contact, and preventative information (information about backups, policies that keep all special collection materials at least 3 feet above the floor, etc.).

A sample plan follows (much of this is borrowed from the dPlan introduction/scope statement, but some text has been added to include technology in the plan):

> "This disaster plan addresses prevention of and response to emergencies that may affect the library's collections" and technology. In all cases, human safety is always the most important concern. No actions should be taken to protect or salvage the collections or the technology that might endanger human safety, and damaged collections and technology should be addressed only after injuries have been attended to and the building is secure for people to enter.
>
> This plan focuses on the most likely risks the library faces: (1) minor flooding from roof or pipe leaks, due to the age of the roof and the previous problem with pipe leakage on the first floor, (2) flooding or other damage from severe winter weather, and (3) fire, due to the lack of a fire suppression system in the building. Preventive actions are covered in the appendices of this plan, while response and recovery steps are addressed in the body of the plan.
>
> Staff should be able to manage small water emergencies (one stack range or less in the general collection) using basic "removal of materials and shutting down of technology prior to moving to a dry area." If a small-scale emergency involves the special collections, outside consultation with preservation professional is advisable (see Appendix A for contact information). If a small-scale emergency involves mission-critical technology, outside consultation with a vendor is advisable (see Appendix A for contact information).
>
> For larger-scale damage, additional assistance and a more detailed plan for recovery will be needed. Depending on the type of emergency, staff will need to secure the building, assess the damage as soon as the building is secure and safe and begin restoration procedures. These

procedures include removing collections from water onto higher ground as is possible, visually inspecting technology to determine if it's been wet (then allowing to dry and turning that technology on to see if it's recoverable) and checking on backups to make sure they are accessible if needed. "See the Appendices for supplies, services, record-keeping forms, emergency funds, insurance information, etc. Especially in a large-scale emergency, it is crucial to be aware of the library's salvage priorities, which focus on the special collections materials and hard-to-replace materials in the general collection. In any emergency, be sure to determine whether salvage, reformatting, replacement, or discard is the proper course of action." (Northeast Document Conservation Center & Massachusetts Board of Library Commissioners, 2006)

Of course, you can always add more as needed for your situation, but the bare bones above would work for many small libraries with minimal technology and relatively few risks. Another option that might be useful is to create a worksheet from the above statement with the opening paragraph staying the same, but the rest of the plan in worksheet format.

This plan focuses on the most likely risks the library faces:

1) _____

2) _____

3) _____

For small-scale emergencies, staff should:

_____

_____

_____

_____

For large-scale emergencies, staff should:

_____

_____

_____

_____

Vendors for technology recovery are:

Company: _____ Phone: _____

Company: _____ Phone: _____

Vendors for collection recovery are:

Company: _____ Phone: _____

Company: _____ Phone: _____

List of Appendices:

Appendix A: _____

Appendix B: _____

Appendix C: _____

This would be useful for quickly changing circumstances and for groups of libraries wanting to work on their disaster plans together—having forms to fill out can be less intimidating than having to write full paragraphs. The samples for the medium- and large-sized libraries will be in standard narrative form, but they can also be adjusted to worksheet form if that works.

SAMPLES FOR MEDIUM LIBRARIES

For medium-sized libraries, you would recreate the plan sample from above as an introductory statement for your plan, then finish the plan with more concrete procedures for securing what is likely a more complicated technology landscape. After the introduction, you can add the response team's contact information in a simple table format:

In Table 7.1, the name, role in the library and role in the plan recovery process, and address and phone contact information are presented where they can be easily found. In today's cell phone environment, it's possible to also have information texted (using SMS messaging) to phones instead of calling. This can be faster than calling each person and explaining the situation individually—group texting is a feature most phones today have.

Table 7.1 Contact Information

Name	Role	Address	Phone
Ingrid Tesh	IT Director / Plan Lead	1234 Main St. Yourtown, ST, 55555	(555) 555-5555 (SMS capable)
Carey Bishop	Circulation Manager / Secondary Lead/Collection Specialist	4321 Main St. Yourtown, ST, 55555	(555) 666-6666 (SMS capable)
Josh Waylan	Facilities Manager / Building Specialist	5678 High St. Yourtown, ST, 55555	(555) 777-7777 (No SMS)

Table 7.2 Inventory Table

Item	Use	Office Location	Estimated Cost
Desktop Computer—Dell	Ingrid	IT Office	$1100
Desktop Computer—Dell (2)	Circulation	Circulation Desk	$800
Laptop	Josh	Mail Room	$1200
Server	File Server	IT Office	$2400

After the contact information, medium-sized libraries should have a current inventory list included in their plan. This can be something simple—just an acknowledgement of the machines that the library owns so that in the case of a major disaster, the response team knows what to look for. You can also put this information in the plan in a table format (see Table 7.2).

This can be useful for both insurance purposes and for identifying and replacing computers as needed after a disaster.

The prevention part of the plan can be added here or in an appendix, but should include at least a statement of how you plan to prevent risk as much as possible:

Fire

There are sprinkler systems throughout the library that will be activated when the smoke detector and fire alarm both go off. Fire extinguishers are in every office and public area of the library, with 2 in the larger areas (adult circulation, children's circulation).

Flood

All computer equipment is on platforms that raise them at least 6 inches off the ground to avoid damage from small floods. If computer equipment is damaged in a larger flood, all computers are backed up to the central file server which is backed up to a cloud service (details of the cloud service would go here—what the name of the service is at least should be documented in the prevention section).

Large Storms

All servers are on UPS (uninterruptible power supply) units that will keep the machines running for at least one hour to allow time for employees to come in and shut them down properly. All desktop and laptop computers are plugged into surge protectors that have active warranties for damage during an electrical storm.

For the "Response and Recovery" sections, a quick checklist on how to recover backups from your cloud backup site and information on replacing computers is useful:

Response

Either Ingrid or Carey must be notified as soon as possible after a disaster. Once the library has been deemed safe, they should go in and assess the damage to the library's technology.

Recovery

Backups are stored at Cloud Vendor's site at http://www.example.com/backups and the recovery process includes (insert checklist of data recovery steps here). Individual computers should be assessed and if no longer operational can be replaced using the emergency technology fund through our preferred vendor Big Computer Sales Company. Recovering server information is the first priority, individual computers and printers/fax machines/phones are handled after the server is back up and running.

"Supplies and Services" can be just a list of the services you would use (such as the Big Computer Sales Company) in recovery efforts. The "Staff Training" section should include:

Staff Training

All IT staff should be trained in backup recovery processes and the IT Director and at least one IT staff member should be knowledgeable about how to order and provision new computers for replacements. One staff member from each department should be certified in CPR and general first aid processes.

Each year, all staff will be asked to read and sign a copy of this disaster plan, indicating that they are aware of the prevention, response, and recovery procedures outlined within it.

The sample given above is still a fairly basic example of a disaster plan, but it is a start for most medium-sized libraries. More details and more information is always better, but with just the basics outlined, as above, staff will have a good start on how to recover from a disaster.

SAMPLES FOR LARGE LIBRARIES

Large libraries will need a large plan, just because there is more technology in the library to protect and recover. Most plans for libraries that are fairly large (more than 100 or 150 employees) will require some kind of table of contents that will help people find the information they need quickly. A sample of one that would be useful (without page numbers, though those would be helpful in a real plan) is included here:

Table of Contents—Large Library Disaster Plan

1. Organizational Information

    a. Administration contacts

    b. Disaster planning team contact information

    c. Disaster recovery team contact information

2. Scope and Goals

    a. Scope

        i. Likely disasters

        ii. What is covered

        iii. What is not covered

    b. Goals

        i. Priorities

        ii. Prevention

        iii. Recovery procedures for each type of disaster (this would be pointers to later on in the plan)

3. Prevention

    a. Technological prevention

        i. Backups

        ii. Monitoring and virus scanning

        iii. Network monitoring schedule

    b. Human prevention

        i. Staff training

        ii. Security policies and procedures

    c. Facilities prevention

        i. Fire prevention

        ii. Flood prevention

        iii. Electrical disruption prevention

        iv. Opening and closing procedures for protection

            1. Staff protection procedures

            2. Technology protection procedures

4. **Response and Recovery**

   a. Response procedures

      i. Contacts

         1. Police, fire, emergency
         2. Staff
         3. City/county officials

      ii. Checklist of to-dos after all-clear is given
      iii. Evaluation of technology losses

   b. Recovery

      i. Backups
      ii. Hot site or cloud sites for recovery of lost technology
      iii. Checklist for what information should be gathered

         1. Financial
         2. Insurance
         3. Operational
         4. Personnel

5. **Supplies and Services**

   a. Supplies

      i. Lists with locations
      ii. Where to get more supplies (vendors)

   b. Services

      i. Vendor list (with prices and contract information)

6. **Staff Training**

   a. Training plans and procedures
   b. Checklist for staff training completion

7. **Distribution/Review/Updating (likely just one page with dates and signature lines)**

   a. Date distributed
   b. Persons distributed to
   c. Date last reviewed
   d. Date of next update

Using the suggestions in Chapter 6 and earlier in this chapter, you should be able to come up with a pretty complete and useful disaster plan following the table of contents given above.

A successful disaster plan is one that works to help you recover your assets after a disaster. That could mean a lot of different things to a lot of different types of libraries. The samples given here are very much technology related, a really successful plan will have plans for the staff and the materials as well, though those kinds of plans are mostly outside the scope of this book. While using a cloud-based service to help you create and maintain your disaster plan as well as carry out the procedures laid out within it, just having thought of what your library might do in case of a disaster will put you ahead, no matter how you lay out those thoughts. The process of going through the disaster planning brainstorming and thinking will help your library immensely—no formal template or structure will make up for the thinking part, though it may make it more easily used after the disaster happens if it's thoughtfully laid out and easy to use.

Chapter 8

Wrapping It All Up

No plan will be useful if you don't make people aware of it! While the act of planning is useful in and of itself, it's only really useful for the people who are involved. A good disaster plan needs to be available and made use of by a wide range (if not all) of your staff to be sure that it will be thought of, grabbed, and used when the need arises. It's also a good idea to get the plan and its procedures out of the building—not just physically on paper or on the website but also in the minds of citizens of your area who might be in the library when the disaster happens or who might be affected by the disaster as well. Everyone in your community should know that you have a plan if disaster should strike, though not everyone needs to know the nitty-gritty details, of course! You should have the plan available and consider it as one of those very important documents that should be protected by the LOCKSS method of document preservation (Lots of Copies Keep Stuff Safe—a full discussion of this is found in Chapter 2). Finally, you need to revisit the plan regularly. Circumstances and technologies change rapidly and an out-of-date plan is far less than useful in the case of a disaster!

PRESENTING THE PLAN

The more eyes that are on your plan, the more people are thinking about it, the better. Your plan should be very familiar to your staff, of course, but you need to make sure you have more than just the library's staff aware of it. Leaders in the community should be familiar with your plan and how it might affect their organizations, especially if you are a designated safety center. Some libraries are the official warming or cooling centers in their towns or have information on evacuation routes for the town, which means they stay open during weather-related disasters in order to provide a heated or cooled environment for people who might not otherwise have access. If that is the case for your library, or if you are an officially designated emergency shelter of any sort, the community you serve should be aware of this—it could save lives in an emergency if people know where to go. There are a number of ways to let your community know about your disaster plans and how you can help the whole community in the case of a major disaster in your area.

GO OUT INTO THE COMMUNITY AND TALK ABOUT IT!

One of the best ways to let folks know about your disaster plans and how they will be useful for the community is to get out into the community and talk. Many community organizations will be happy to give a representative from the library a few minutes of time during a meeting or service or other gathering to talk about how the library can help keep their members safe in a disaster.

While you don't need to be a polished presenter to give this information out during meetings, you should practice in low-stress situations first (talk to friends and groups of staff to get some practice in both what you have to say and how you want to say it). You should have visual aids (a PowerPoint presentation or other kind of visual helper) for those times when you can use them, but be prepared to speak without them as well—not every venue to which you will be invited will be set up for that kind of thing. You should prepare a handout of the basic information you plan to give and have it ready to go at a moment's notice—you never know when you'll be asked to speak! The presentation itself should be adaptable to your audience's needs—there should be a 5-minute version, a 30-minute version, and an hour long version that you can produce at a moment's notice when an invitation comes along. It would also be a good idea to highlight any resources your library has on the process of disaster planning—books from your collection, databases with information to which you may subscribe, and any other resources you may have collected in the process of creating your own plan. The discussion of your disaster plan will likely spark interest in other groups to do the same thing, and positioning your library as a place to get information on how to do that will go a long way to helping your community think of your library as their go-to place for information of all kinds.

Deciding who will speak about the library is important, too. You need to have someone with some authority who knows the library well and can answer questions as they come up in the presentation. An administrator and at least a couple of branch/department-level managers should be ready to go for big libraries. If you have a couple of people who are comfortable talking about the plan and who can answer questions about it, even for smaller libraries, that's ideal. The more available you are and the more people you have to schedule, the easier it will be to get your message out in front of the community. For smaller libraries, this will likely fall on the director to do most of the time.

The final part of this is getting invitations to speak. You will need to get the word out and be willing to talk up the service to anyone you can corner in order to get those invitations—they won't come without your library doing a bit of leg work first. Start with community service organizations like the Lion's Club or the Rotary Club. If there is a Masonic Lodge, Eagles club, or VFW of any sort in your town, go talk to them about coming to an upcoming meeting to discuss disaster preparedness and the library. You should be in contact with fire houses, police stations, and hospitals as well to be sure that they are aware of your plan and can, hopefully, help you implement it in a disaster. Don't forget about religious organizations, too—churches can invite you to speak during services, religious groups like Knights of Columbus can have you come to their meetings to speak and religious service organizations may be not only willing to have you speak to their members, but might be willing to work with you during the disaster as well. Civic organizations like the Chamber of Commerce or other business organizations in your area would be a good target as well. Get out there and network to find out what kind of organizations are in your town and who might be open to having the library come around to talk about disaster plans to them.

HAVE A PARTY!

While going out to talk about your disaster plan will be an efficient way to get the word out to the community, letting patrons and interested community members know in a more informal and fun way may be a good way to get word of mouth about your plan going in your community. Having a "disaster plan kickoff" party, where you serve refreshments and provide information about the plan and how it will affect patrons can be a fun way to get the word out. Focusing on the positives (what you are doing to avoid risk, how the plan helps to keep disasters from happening, etc.) will keep the party from getting too serious while also letting your community know that you are working to keep materials and staff safe. While you are at it, ask the people who show up for invitations to their favorite community, religious, or service group's next meeting!

This is a good way to get some practice for speaking outside the library, too. The folks who make a point to come to a presentation at the library are going to be both interested and less critical of the presentation style—but they may have some good tips for when you go out to talk about the plan to others. This is also a good way to ask for feedback for the plan. As you present the general outlines, people who are listening may have ideas for other ways you can prevent, monitor for, or recover from a disaster. Even if they have nothing to add to the plan itself, they may have ideas for how to get the word out, beyond personal talks, parties, and cloud-based marketing!

MARKET THE PLAN

Use the cloud to help market your plan as well. Create a marketing plan that includes your website as well as local news outlets. Make sure the plan is easily accessible on your site and is announced on your social networks, with links to the plan on your site, of course. Provide marketing materials such as press releases and succinct overviews of the plan for local media. The easier you make it for them to report on your plan, the more likely it is that they will do it. Provide contact links for in-person interviews in those materials, as well. TV stations like to have a real person talking about the subjects they cover, so you want to be accessible to them if they come calling.

Check to see if there are local repositories of government documents in your area. A national one that is available, though not used as much as it was a few years ago, is the Library Success Wiki (http://libsuccess.org/Disaster_ and_Emergency_Planning) — create an account and start adding your plans to the wiki—it will both help folks who are looking for example plans in the future and it will give you another outlet to publicize your plan.

One thing to remember, though, is the personal information included in your plan. If you have contact information for individuals (such as phone numbers and addresses) in your plan, you will definitely want to clean the plan up before making it public and marketing it. While the copies that are stored locally or in private cloud accounts for the library can, and should, include the contact information for key personnel, the plans that are being made public should not. Some people don't even want their e-mail addresses to be posted to publicly accessible websites, so be aware of the needs of your key personnel when it comes to posting this information for the world to see.

STORING THE PLAN
On Paper

There should be paper copies kept at both key personnel's houses and at various places around the city or community that your library serves. If there is a large-scale disaster that takes out electricity or the Internet in your community, it would be handy to have the paper copy at hand for everyone who needs it. One thing to work out is how to indicate where those paper copies have been stored. This is especially vital if the disaster is truly large and many of the community's buildings and common areas have been destroyed.

Everyone in the administrative department—not just the director, but business office staff and HR personnel—should have a copy of the plan at their home. Every person on the disaster recovery team should have a copy at their home as well. For smaller libraries, where the administrative staff and the disaster recovery staff are all concentrated in one, or maybe two, people, pull in friends and volunteers to store copies at their houses, too. If the library has a vehicle (or vehicles—including bookmobiles), store copies of the plan in that as well. While nothing will survive an event like Yellowstone erupting (at least if you are in the blast radius), the more areas in which your plan can be stashed, the better off you'll be. The downside to this, of course, is that when the plan is updated and revised, new copies should be sent out to replace the old in all the various locations that the plan resides. Be sure to update the lists of people who have the plan (something that should be included in the plan itself and possibly in a document on the cloud, as well) as needed, too. Knowing just exactly where the plan is after a disaster can help speed up your implementation of the recovery parts of the plan.

The community's common areas (city hall, county courthouse, administrative building at a college, home office for special corporate libraries, etc.) should also house a copy of the library's disaster plan. If your administrative and plan teams are small, you can use the homes of some of the officials of your community to store those plans as well! If you have a multijurisdictional library—one that spans multiple cities or counties or campus locations—be sure to deposit a copy in the common area of each individual city, county, or campus in the system. This will really help to distribute the copies widely and will definitely keep things safe through the LOCKSS principle.

Keeping track of these far-flung plans, however, can be a nightmare—especially at revision time. You could add to the plan a page that lists all the locations the plan has been sent to and make sure it's included in every copy sent out and stored both physically and in the cloud. This kind of log will help you when the time comes to either find a copy in a disaster or replace or add to plans at revision/rewriting time.

In the Cloud

There are a number of places in the cloud that you can use to store your disaster plan. In your cloud areas that you already have (Amazon, Google Docs, MS 360, Dropbox, etc.) and in repositories of plans—use wikis such as the Library Success Wiki mentioned in the previous section or create your own. This is both a marketing and LOCKSS style storage technique! Don't forget though, unless you are storing your plan in a private, password protected cloud that you control, you need to clean up the personal information from contact lists and such before you post the plan.

If you have an account with Dropbox, Box.net, or any of the other personal cloud services, use it to store a copy of your plan. Make sure that your key personnel have access to this account but that it's also well-protected with a strong password to help keep the information in it safe from prying eyes. The same thing can be done with an Amazon, Google, Microsoft, or other cloud services. If you have space online, use it to store a copy of your plan and make that space accessible to everyone who needs it. Often you can share individual files with people without having to share everything in the account—Dropbox and Box.net work this way—so take advantage of that feature if you can to spread the ability to access the plan in an emergency around as needed.

Wikis and other file repositories are useful for storing plans and other public government documents as well. As the public library, you may be best positioned to create and maintain a government document repository that includes the text of local ordinances, bylaws for public organizations, and minutes from local open meetings—as well as strategic and disaster plans from a wide range of public organizations, including yours. As an academic or special library, you may already have something like this going for your business, university, or college community—be sure to add your plan to it!

REVISITING THE PLAN: REVISE OR REWRITE?

Every so often, you should revisit your plan. This should, if you have been following the advice in this book, already be built into the schedule around the plan and you should already be revisiting the plan every time you test it, at least, and every few years as well—independent of the testing process. When should you revise the plan and when should you ditch it and completely rewrite it, though? This question will depend entirely on the environment of your library.

If you have had a major change in the library's environment—especially the technological environment—it may be time to rewrite the plan from scratch. A new building or even just a new server room and network configuration would be cause to have to rewrite most of your disaster planning procedures. As more and more of the services on which your library relies move to the cloud, there will come a time when you no longer have a local server at all—or you are down to one local server instead of a bank of them—and the technological environment of your library will be sufficiently changed to require a whole new plan to protect it.

Administrative changes might trigger a whole new rewrite as well. A new director or a change in the board/trustees might make it necessary to make changes to how the plan is carried out that could result in needing to rewrite the whole thing. If a new director comes in and makes big changes to personnel or procedures or if a new board member has some concerns with the current plan, it would be advisable to weigh the considerable costs of rewriting the plan with the only slightly less considerable costs of major revisions to the plan. Either way, when big changes happen in the library, the disaster plan should be considered—do those changes affect the way the plan will be administered?

Revising brings its own challenges. How much to revise should be clearly laid out in the beginning of the project (if using traditional project management techniques, setting the scope statement early is a must in this case). The planning team should go through each section individually to make the changes called for by the change in the organization (whether that is personnel changes or procedural changes or technological changes) and then do a final read-through of the whole plan as a group to make sure the plan is internally consistent and that all changes that are needed have been made. Your team is going to want to stress accuracy and completeness during this process, just like they did in the original writing of the plan!

Each time the plan is tested, a small revision process should happen. Even if nothing has changed in the library's environment, what was learned during testing will suggest changes and updates that need to be made to the plan. Rarely will you have a plan that is perfect to the point of being able to learn nothing and add nothing after a full-scale test project has been carried out. Each testing step should have a "lessons learned" section in the documentation—use that to do small revisions to the plan.

After every revision—no matter how small—the plan needs to be redistributed. New paper copies need to go out to everyone who holds a copy of the older one and new electronic copies need to be uploaded to every place that the original plan was deposited. For very small revisions, publicity about the change could be limited to just staff members and maybe some affected community members. Larger revisions should be publicized more widely, in the same ways that the original plan was marketed to your community.

Following the advice in this book should help you both reduce the risks of a disaster happening (those you can avoid, at least) and make your library come back from a disaster more quickly and with less expense. Disaster plans are sometimes hard to think about—no one wants to consider the effects of a natural disaster or catastrophic accident—but doing the hard work to consider what might happen, how your library can respond to it, and what to do to recover will pay off in the end.

Appendix A: Checklist for Disaster Plans

INSTITUTIONAL INFORMATION

- ☐ Administrative contact information
- ☐ Recovery team contact information
- ☐ Financial and commercial contact information

PREVENTION

- ☐ Backups

  - ✓ Include information on each and every computer/server/device being backed up
  - ✓ Include recovery locations

- ☐ Monitoring

  - ✓ Virus protection
  - ✓ Network monitoring
  - ✓ Firewall monitoring

RESPONSE AND RECOVERY

- ☐ Response

  - ✓ Break down by person responsible
  - ✓ Include step-by-step instructions on who responds and how

- ☐ Recovery

  - ✓ Backup recovery procedures
  - ✓ Virus cleaning procedures
  - ✓ Provisioning new computers/servers procedures

SUPPLIES AND SERVICES

- ☐ Supplies

  - ✓ Include all supplies needed for a disaster (with dates provisioned—useful for yearly checking of expired supplies)
  - ✓ Include lists of supply vendors

☐ Services

    ✓ Contact information for service providers

STAFF TRAINING

☐ Kinds of training needed
☐ Training verification (check off staff training as it is performed)

DISTRIBUTION

☐ Where copies are kept
☐ Date of last (few) tests/revision
☐ Signature pages for administrative sign-off

Appendix B: Checklist for Evaluating Cloud Vendors

GENERAL QUESTIONS FOR CLOUD VENDORS

- ☐ Bandwidth requirements

- ☐ Pricing structure and payment options

- ☐ Skills needed

- ☐ Reliability guarantees

- ☐ Recovery timeframes

- ☐ Scalability of service

- ☐ How do you test your services?

- ☐ Do you use hot sites or other guarantees that you will bring up in a major disaster? (what's their disaster plan?)

- ☐ What hardware/software requirements do your service have?

- ☐ Customer referrals (though you should go looking for these independently of your vendor, too!)

Bibliography

"A Public Trust At Risk: The Heritage Health Index Report on the State of America's Collections." (2005, May 1). Heritage Preservation. Retrieved from https://www.pcah.gov/sites/default/files/HHIsummary.pdf.

Buser, R. A., Massis, B. E., and Pollack, M. (2014). *Project Management for Libraries: A Practical Approach.* Jefferson, NC: McFarland.

Northeast Document Conservation Center and Massachusetts Board of Library Commissioners. (2006). dPlan. Retrieved July 4, 2017, from http://dplan.org/scop/disasterplan.asp.

Prince, Brian. (2012). "Security Not Keeping Pace with Consumerization of IT, Forrester Research Finds." *Security Week*, 9–24. Retrieved from http://www.securityweek.com/security-not-keeping-pace-consumerization-it-forrester-research-finds.

Vermont Council on Rural Development (VCRD). (2014). "Final Report of VCRD's Vermont Digital Economy Project." Retrieved from http://bit.ly/VDEPreport.

Index

About the Author

ROBIN M. HASTINGS is the Library Services Consultant at the Northeast Kansas Library System (NEKLS) in Lawrence, KS. She has been working in libraries for 17 years and is a prolific writer and speaker on technology in libraries. She has written three books, several articles for library trade journals, and a Library Technology Report. She has presented at conferences and workshops around the world. Her first book, *Microblogging and Livestreaming for Libraries*—one of the original Tech Set books—won Best Library Literature (as part of the set) in 2011.